illumibugs

WIDE EYED EDITIONS

by

Carnovsky

written by

Barbara Taylor

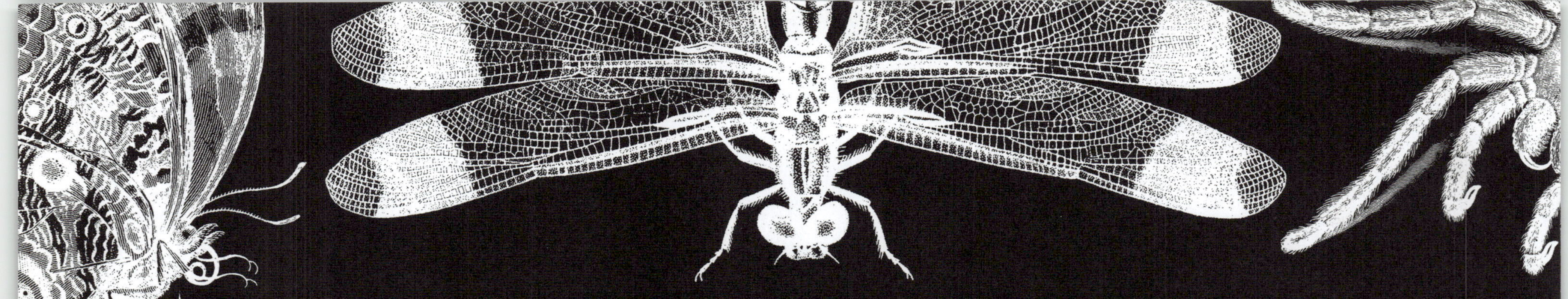

welcome to the world of bugs

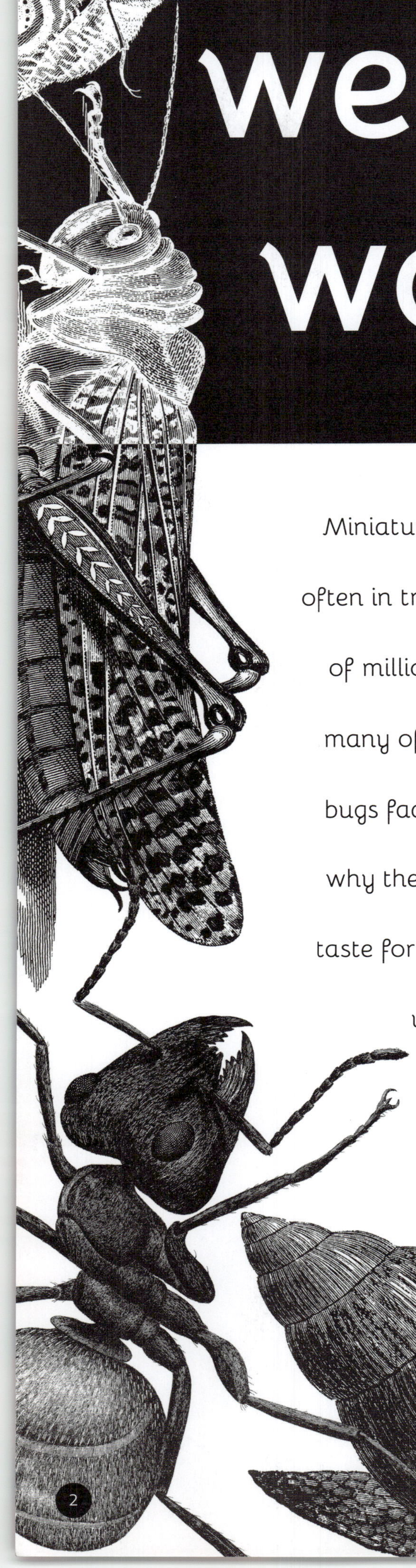

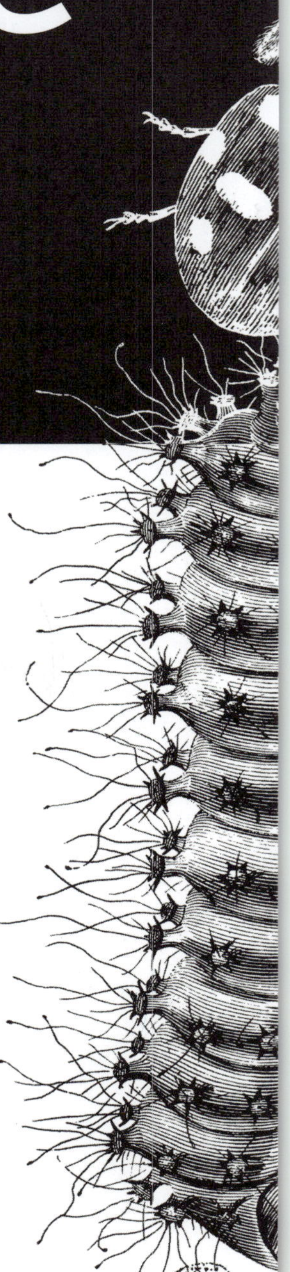

Miniature in scale, but leading incredible and surprising lives, bugs live everywhere, often in truly mind-boggling numbers. They have survived on our planet for hundreds of millions of years. Get ready to reveal the amazing world of these mini-beasts, many of which look like alien monsters from another galaxy. Dare to meet scary bugs face-to-face on the observation deck and explore the species guide to learn why they have evolved cunning disguises, deadly weapons, hairy legs, and even a taste for blood! Travel all over the world to illuminate the secret world of bugs and understand the extraordinary tactics they rely on for their survival.

What will you discover on your bug adventure around the globe?

CONTENTS

Travel across the world's continents to take a closer look at the fantastic creepy crawlies living on our planet today and in the prehistoric past.

HOW TO USE THIS BOOK

BUG WORLD

Visit a ***continent***, an ***underwater*** world, or time-travel into ***the past*** to discover key facts about the habitats and their bugs.

THE OBSERVATION DECK

Step on to the ***observation deck***. Tread carefully and watch out for flying insects, stinging scorpions, and giant creepy crawlies...

SPECIES GUIDE

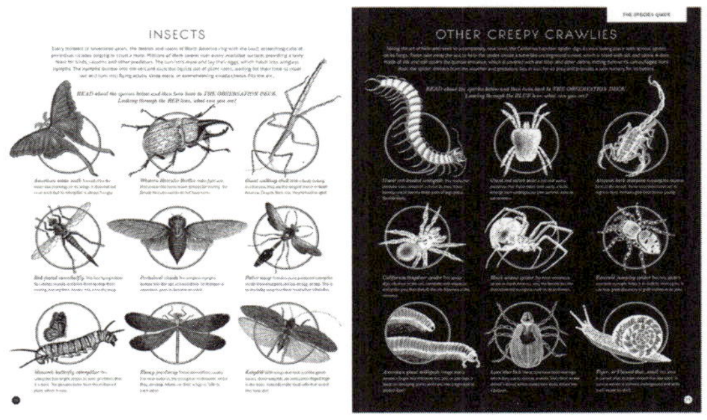

Find out the name of each species and learn more about the features that help it to survive in the ***species guide***.

Use the ***red*** lens to reveal the INSECTS

Look through the ***green*** lens to highlight the PLANT LIFE.

Look through the ***blue*** lens to focus on the OTHER CREEPY CRAWLIES.

FAMILY TREE

Bugs lived on our planet long before dinosaurs or people, and insects were the first creatures to use their fragile wings to take to the air. Today, bugs make up more than ninety percent of all the different kinds of animals on Earth. The greatest variety of bugs live in the hot, wet rainforests of South America, but bugs survive on all continents, including the icy Arctic, and the dry African and Australian deserts. To a scientist, bugs are a particular group of insects with piercing and sucking mouthparts, such as cicadas. In this book, we have used a more informal definition of bugs, which includes all the insect groups, as well as other land and freshwater creepy crawlies, from spiders, scorpions, and shrimps to centipedes, snails, and worms. Bugs play many essential roles in the survival of life on our planet. They are vital links in food chains, pollinate plants, and recycle animal poop and other natural waste. Sadly, many bugs are threatened with extinction.

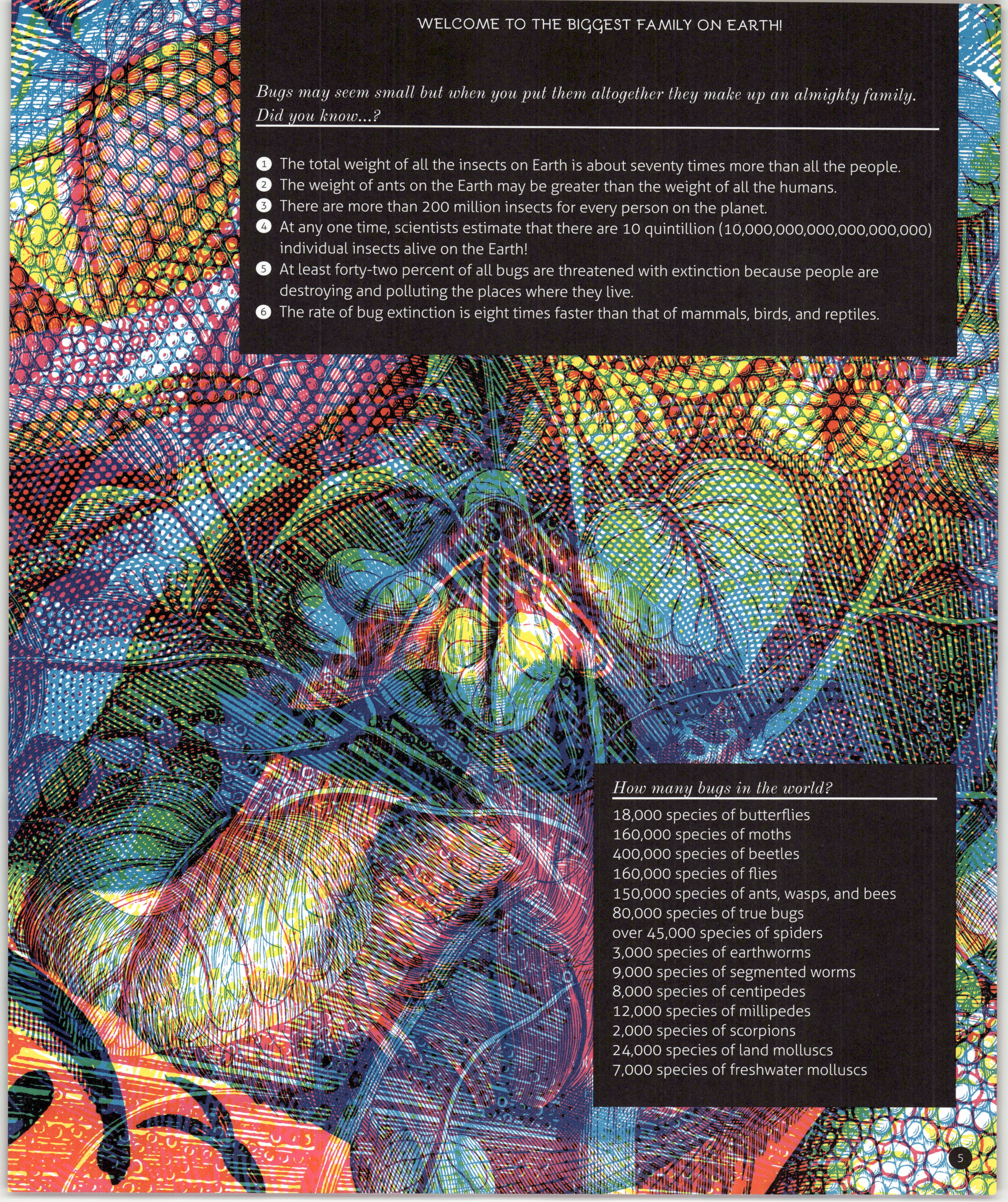

WELCOME TO THE BIGGEST FAMILY ON EARTH!

Bugs may seem small but when you put them altogether they make up an almighty family. Did you know...?

1. The total weight of all the insects on Earth is about seventy times more than all the people.
2. The weight of ants on the Earth may be greater than the weight of all the humans.
3. There are more than 200 million insects for every person on the planet.
4. At any one time, scientists estimate that there are 10 quintillion (10,000,000,000,000,000,000) individual insects alive on the Earth!
5. At least forty-two percent of all bugs are threatened with extinction because people are destroying and polluting the places where they live.
6. The rate of bug extinction is eight times faster than that of mammals, birds, and reptiles.

How many bugs in the world?

18,000 species of butterflies
160,000 species of moths
400,000 species of beetles
160,000 species of flies
150,000 species of ants, wasps, and bees
80,000 species of true bugs
over 45,000 species of spiders
3,000 species of earthworms
9,000 species of segmented worms
8,000 species of centipedes
12,000 species of millipedes
2,000 species of scorpions
24,000 species of land molluscs
7,000 species of freshwater molluscs

INSECTS

Millions of different kinds of insects live on our planet. They include beautiful butterflies, speedy flies and buzzing bees, but the biggest group of insects are beetles. There are so many different kinds of them that one in every four animals on Earth is a beetle! The features that all insects share in common are six legs and three body parts, and most insects have one or two pairs of wings. Insects use two feelers, called antennae, to touch and smell their surroundings.

READ about the species below and then turn back to THE OBSERVATION DECK. Looking through the RED lens, what can you see?

Mantids Often camouflaged to look like leaves, twigs or flowers, mantids have big eyes and bendy necks to spot their prey, and long front legs to seize it!

Flies These insects have only one pair of wings. Their back wings are just thin threads with a club on the end, which help with balance and steering.

Butterflies and moths These insects have a long, hollow feeding tube (called a proboscis) and dust-like scales on their wide, flat wings.

Beetles Beetles have biting and chewing jaws. Their front wings form thick, hard covers, which protect their delicate flying wings underneath.

Ants, wasps and bees Ants, some types of bees and a few kinds of wasps, live in large colonies. Bees and wasps have see-through wings, most ants do not have wings.

Grasshoppers and crickets Huge back legs help them to jump long distances. Grasshoppers have short antennae, while crickets have long antennae.

True bugs These are insects with piercing and sucking mouthparts. True bugs include assassin bugs, cicadas, peanut bugs, water bugs, and aphids (greenfly).

OTHER CREEPY CRAWLIES

From hairy, scary spiders, and deadly scorpions, to slimy slugs, and wriggling worms, each group of creepy crawlies has different features, although none of them can fly. Some, such as centipedes and millipedes, may have hundreds of legs, while spiders and scorpions have eight legs, and worms have no legs at all. Slugs and snails have one big, squishy, slimy "foot" and slide along surfaces. Creepy crawlies protect themselves with poisonous fangs, or stings and some have a hard shell to help them stay safe.

READ about the species below and then turn back to THE OBSERVATION DECK. Looking through the BLUE lens, what can you see?

Scorpions Fierce predators, scorpions have two large pincers to hold, or crush prey and a tail with a sharp sting on the end to inject their prey with venom.

Spiders With eight legs and two body parts, all spiders produce silk, which they use for making webs and wrapping up prey and eggs.

Centipedes and millipedes Both have rings, or segments, which help them to twist and turn. They also have lots of legs. Centipedes are predators, while most millipedes feed on decaying plants.

Crustaceans Crustaceans have a segmented body with more than eight jointed legs and a hard, crusty case. Most live in water and breathe through gills.

Mites and ticks These bugs have two body parts fused into one. Mites are microscopic, whereas most ticks can be seen with the naked eye.

Worms A worm has a long, thin, soft and squishy body. Worms do not have a tough outer body covering, so they use fluids inside their bodies to keep their shape.

Molluscs This group likes the damp, and includes snails, slugs, and mussels. Molluscs have a soft body and many have a hard shell for protection.

NORTH AMERICA

The third largest continent in the world, North America is a continent of contrasts. Its high mountains, warm and cold forests, baking deserts, vast grasslands, and urban environments provide homes for nearly 100,000 species of insects, as well as thousands of other creepy crawlies. The largest of these range from the giant walking stick insect to the giant millipede, while the smallest include tiny mites and blood-sucking ticks. One of the challenges for North American insects and other creepy crawlies is surviving seasonal or daily changes. To avoid cold winters, some of them migrate to warmer places, while others shelter in the soil, in burrows or in rotting wood, or spend the winter hidden away in a resting state as eggs or pupae. Since their bodies lose water easily, insects and other creepy crawlies often avoid hot, dry days by emerging in the cooler, damper night-time air.

WELCOME TO NORTH AMERICA

Continent

North America

Countries

USA, Canada, Mexico

Habitat

Mountain, forests, desert, grassland, scrubland, urban

Size

15.35 million square miles

Who lives here

Hundreds of thousands of bugs live in these three countries, including 18,000 species of bees, wasps, and ants, 30,000 species of beetles, 12,000 species of butterflies and moths, 16,000 species of flies, 5,000 species of true bugs, 4,000 species of spiders, scorpions, mites, and ticks, 1,400 species of millipedes and centipedes and 500 species of snails.

INSECTS

Every thirteen or seventeen years, the forests and towns of North America ring with the loud, screeching calls of periodical cicadas singing to court a mate. Millions of them swarm over every available surface, providing a tasty feast for birds, raccoons, and other predators. The survivors mate and lay their eggs, which hatch into wingless nymphs. The nymphs burrow into the soil and suck the liquids out of plant roots, waiting for their time to crawl out and turn into flying adults. Once more, an overwhelming cicada chorus fills the air...

READ about the species below and then turn back to THE OBSERVATION DECK. Looking through the RED lens, what can you see?

American moon moth Named after the moon-like markings on its wings, it does not eat as an adult but its caterpillar is always hungry.

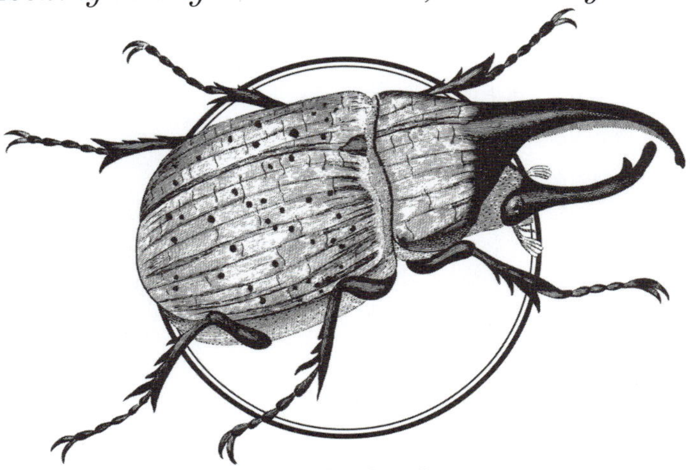

Western Hercules beetle *Males fight with their pincer-like horns to win females for mating. The female Hercules beetle does not have horns.*

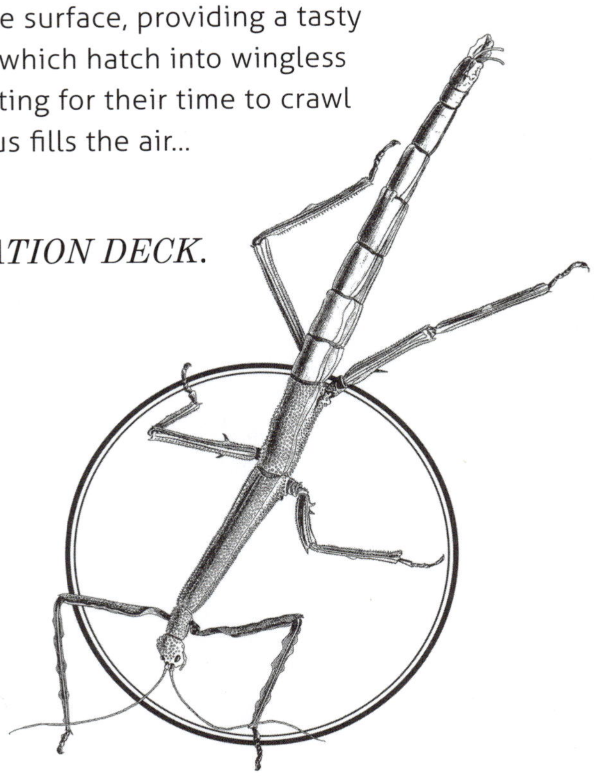

Giant walking stick With a body as long as a banana, they are the longest insect in North America. Despite their size, they're hard to spot.

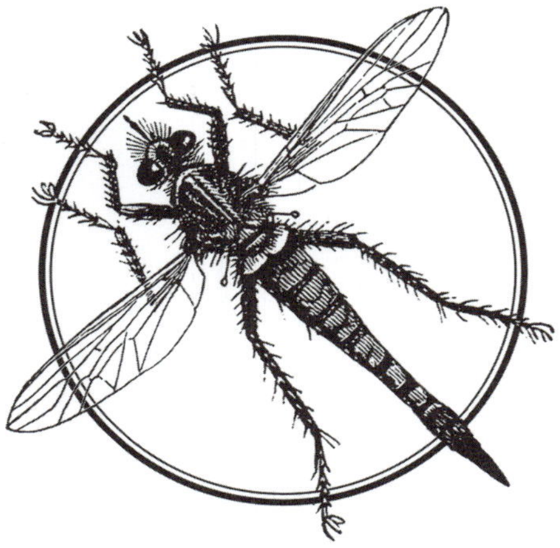

Red-footed cannibalfly This fast flying robber fly catches insects and bites them to stop them moving, turning their insides into a mushy soup.

Periodical cicada The wingless nymphs burrow into the soil and wait there for thirteen or seventeen years to become an adult.

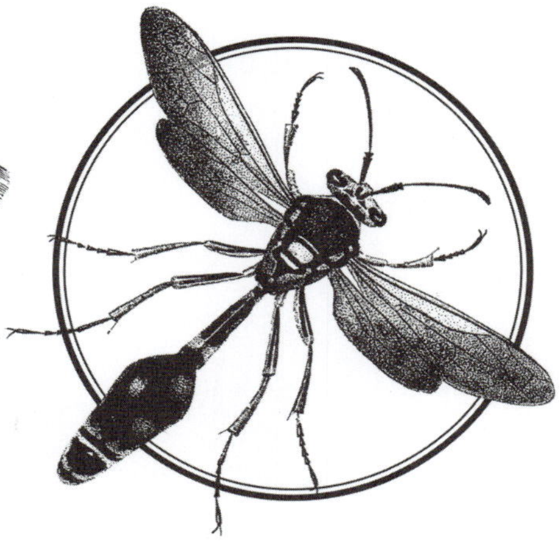

Potter wasp Females put a paralyzed caterpillar inside their mud pots and lay an egg on top. This is so the baby wasp has fresh food when it hatches.

Monarch butterfly caterpillar This caterpillar has bright stripes to warn predators that it is toxic. The poisons come from the milkweed plant, which it eats.

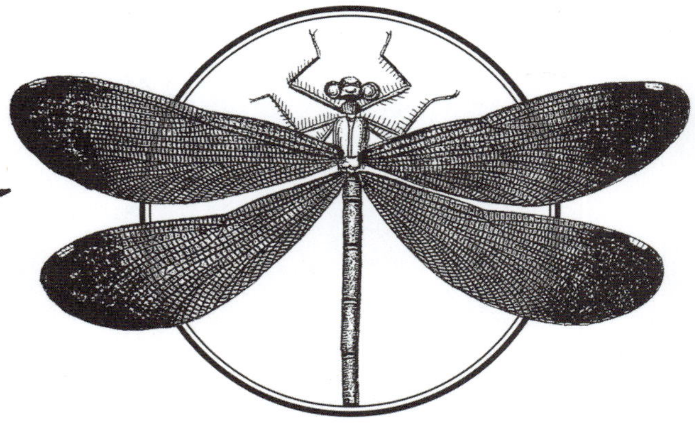

Ebony jewelwing These damselflies usually live near water as the young live underwater while they develop. Adults use their wings to "talk" to each other.

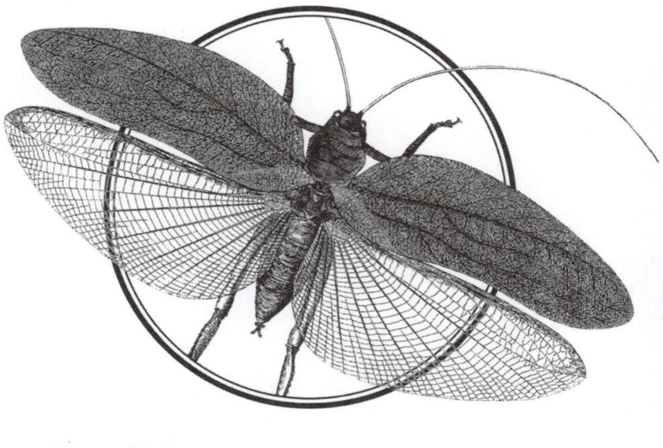

Katydid With wings that look just like green leaves, these katydids are well camouflaged high in the trees. Katydids make loud calls that sound like "Katy-did".

OTHER CREEPY CRAWLIES

Taking the art of hide-and-seek to a completely new level, the California trapdoor spider digs its own hiding place with special spines on its fangs. These rake away the soil to help the spider create a tube-like underground tunnel, which is lined with silk and saliva. A door made of silk and soil covers the burrow entrance, which is covered with leaf litter and other debris. Hiding behind its camouflaged front door, sheltering from the weather and predators, the spider lies in wait for its prey and ensures a safe nursery for its babies.

READ about the species below and then turn back to THE OBSERVATION DECK. Looking through the BLUE lens, what can you see?

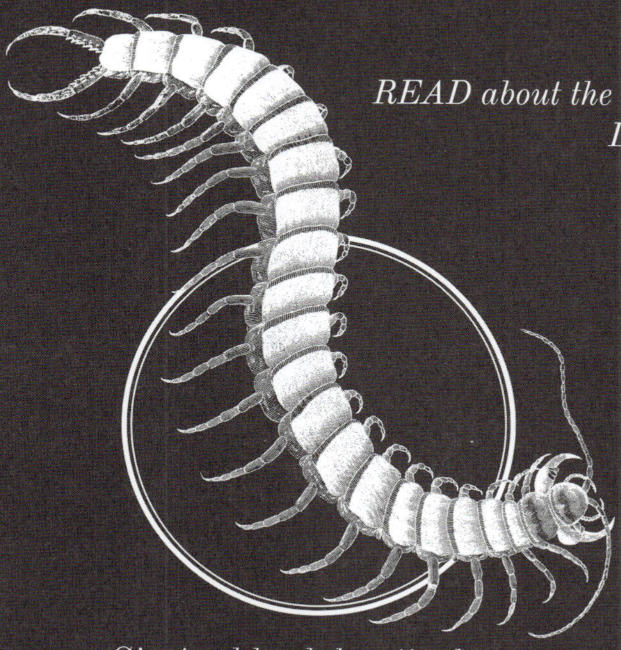

Giant red-headed centipede This nocturnal predator uses venom to subdue its prey. It has twenty-one to twenty-three pairs of legs and a flexible body.

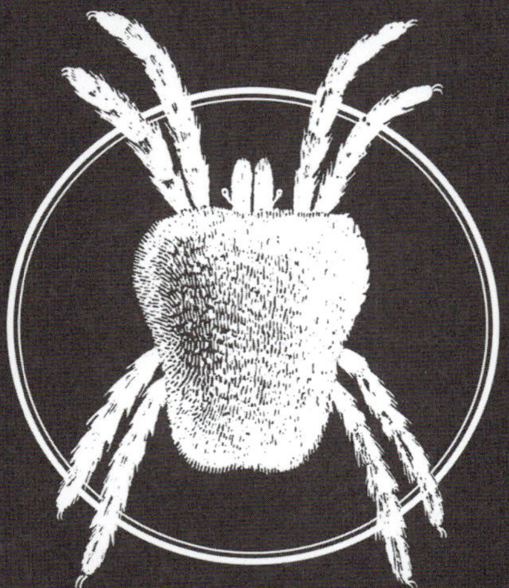

Giant red velvet mite A bright red coat warns predators that these mites taste nasty. Adults emerge from underground after summer rains to eat termites.

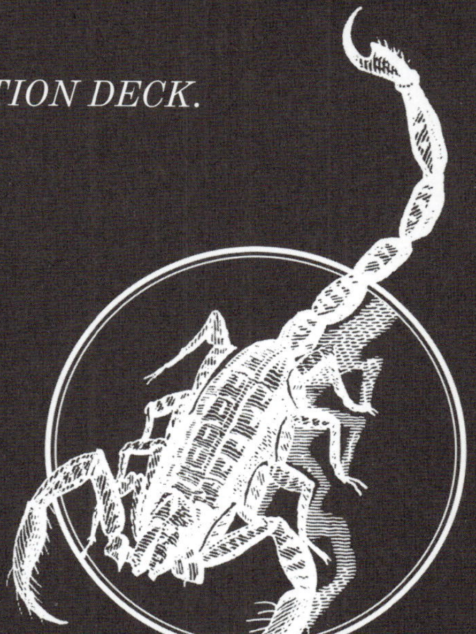

Arizona bark scorpion Avoiding the daytime heat of the desert, these scorpions come out at night to hunt. Females give birth to live young.

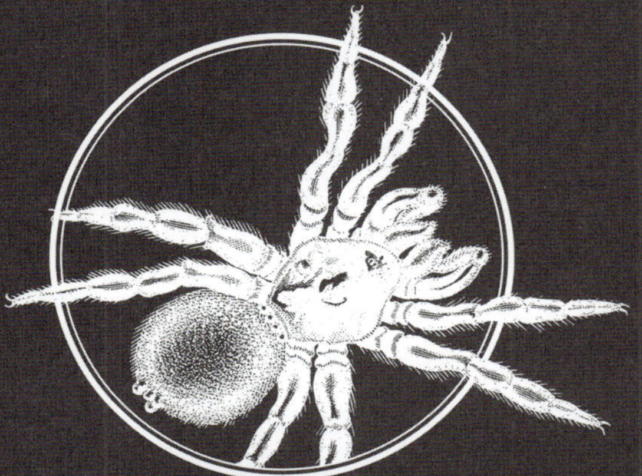

California trapdoor spider This spider digs a burrow in the soil, complete with trapdoor, and grabs prey that disturb the silk tripwires at the entrance.

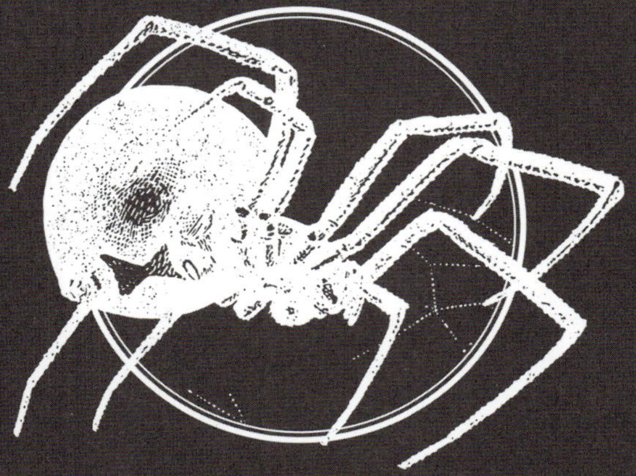

Black widow spider The most venomous spider in North America, only the female has the distinctive red hourglass mark on its abdomen.

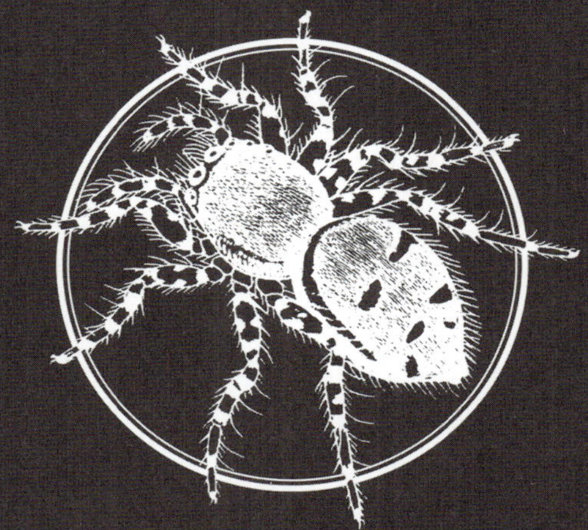

Emerald jumping spider This tiny spider's excellent eyesight helps it to stalk its insect prey. It can leap great distances to grab victims in its jaws.

American giant millipede Longer than a person's finger, this millipede has 300 or 400 legs. It feeds on decaying plants and curls into a tight ball to protect itself.

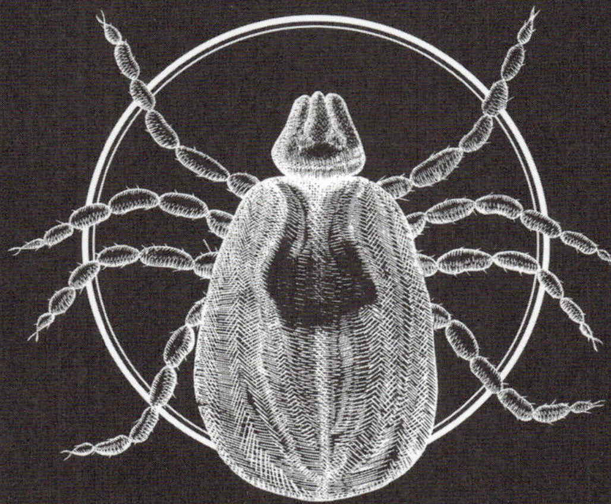

Lone star tick These ticks have hook-like legs which they use to cling to animals. They feed on the animal's blood, which makes their body inflate like a balloon.

Tiger, or Flamed disc, snail This snail is named after its tiger-striped disc-like shell. To survive winter, it burrows underground and seals itself inside its shell.

EUROPE

Europe is the second smallest continent and the only one with no tropical lands. Its bug inhabitants have to survive long, cold winters in the north, and habitats dominated by a human population of almost 750 million. Nearly half of its butterflies and moths are under threat of extinction and in parts of Germany more than three quarters of the flying insects have disappeared. Despite the challenges, a variety of creepy crawlies still thrive in parts of Europe, especially in mountain refuges and in the Mediterranean lands, which come alive with buzzing insects in the hot summer months. Some of the more spectacular European insects include a butterfly named after the Greek Sun god Apollo, the Mountain Apollo, a beetle that makes its own weapons, a wasp that constructs nests from home-made paper and a spider that can change color...

WELCOME TO EUROPE

Continent

Europe

Countries

Forty-four countries, including the regions of: Scandinavia, the Mediterranean, the British Isles, and European Russia

Habitat

Mountain, forest, grassland, scrubland, urban

Size

6.3 million square miles

Who lives here

Despite the threat of extinction due to human overpopulation, you can still find 29,000 species of beetles, up to 20,000 species of bees, wasps, and ants, 9,920 species of butterflies and moths, 19,000 species of flies, 3,000 species of true bugs, 4,500 species of spiders, thirty-five species of scorpions and an impressive 2,000 species of snails!

INSECTS

Lurking unseen in the bushes is an alien predator that looks like a creature from outer space. Suddenly its front legs shoot out to trap its prey behind a wall of deadly spines. The creature bites deeply into its struggling victim and starts to eat it alive. Fortunately for us, this creature is a praying mantis and it's only as long a person's finger – phew, lucky escape!

READ about the species below and then turn back to THE OBSERVATION DECK. Looking through the RED lens, what can you see?

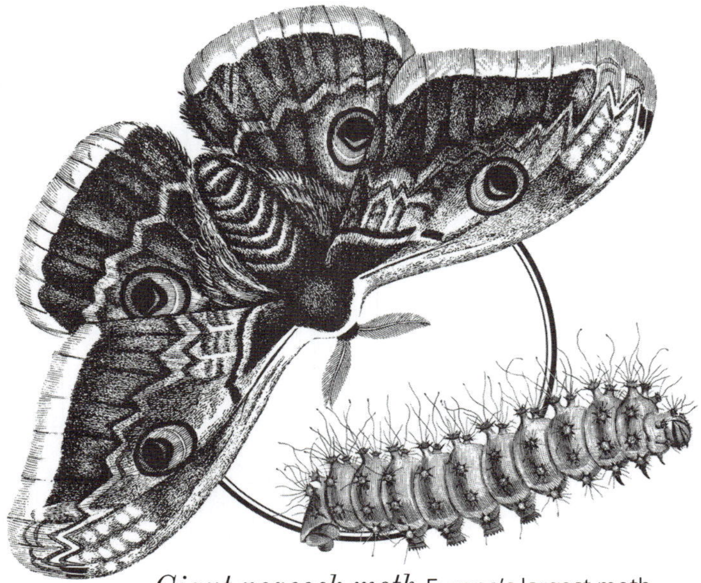

Giant peacock moth Europe's largest moth, it's the size of a small bird. The male's feathery antennae help him to detect a female's scent.

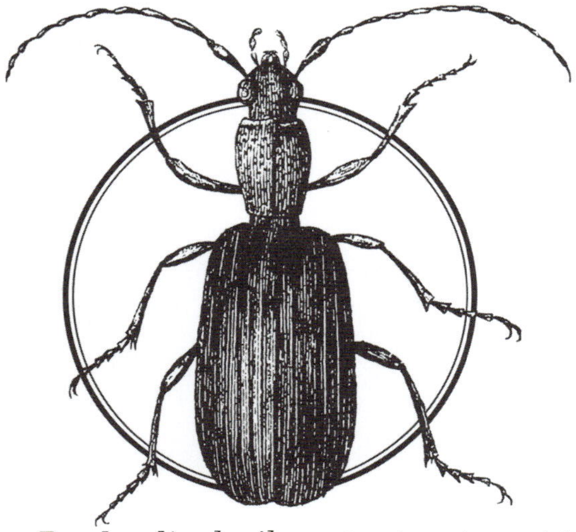

Bombardier beetle This beetle squirts a stinky, boiling hot liquid from its rear end that helps it to escape attackers.

Mountain Apollo butterfly When threatened, the Apollo displays its red eyespots and makes a scratching sound by rubbing its legs under its wings.

Mole cricket Using finger-like projections on its front legs, the heavily armored mole cricket digs burrows in the soil.

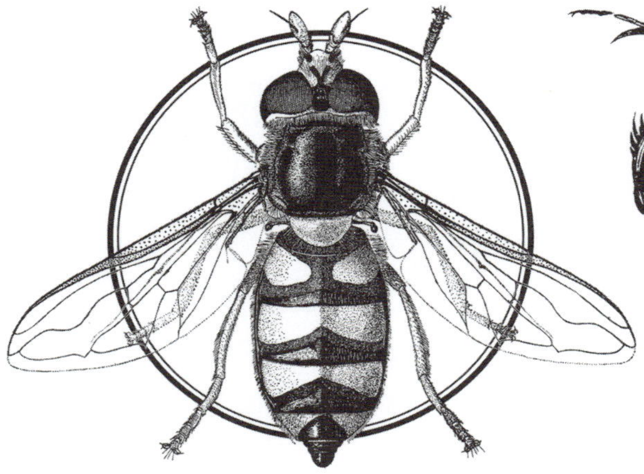

Marmalade hoverfly Hovering silently in mid-air, this hoverfly collects nectar and pollen from flowers, spreading their pollen.

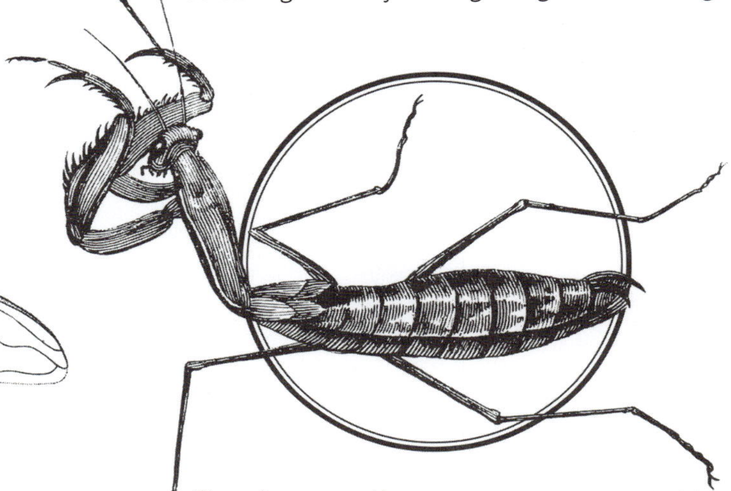

Praying mantis Named after the way it holds its front legs together as if praying, this mantis keeps still and waits to ambush its insect prey.

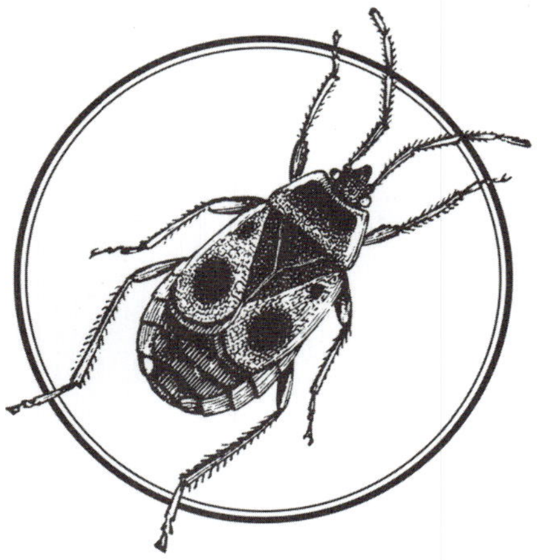

Firebug The red and black colors of firebugs warn predators that they are poisonous. These bugs make poisons from the juices they suck from plants.

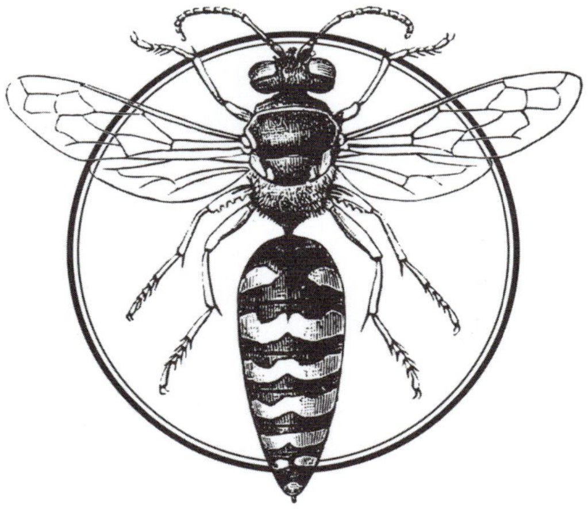

Paper wasp The nests of these paper wasps are built from chewed-up plant materials glued together with saliva.

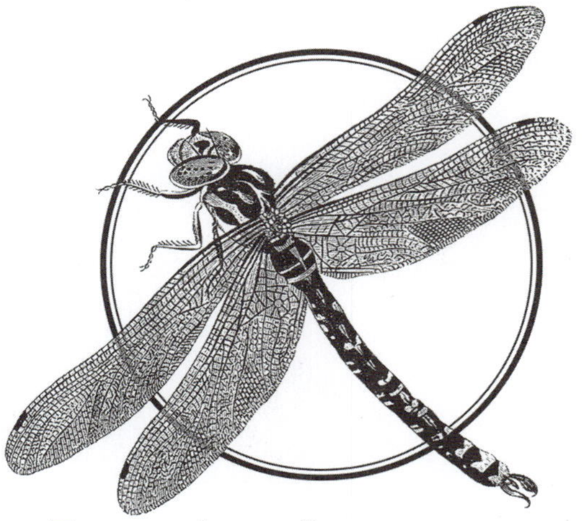

Emperor dragonfly This dragonfly zooms through the air like a tiny helicopter. As it flies, it catches prey with its long, spiky legs.

OTHER CREEPY CRAWLIES

Would you believe that some spiders are caring parents? The female nursery web spider spins a silk cocoon around her eggs and carries this cumbersome bundle around in her fangs for at least five weeks. Before the eggs hatch, the mother builds a silk tent as a nursery and stands guard outside for a week or so to keep the baby spiderlings safe.

READ about the species below and then turn back to THE OBSERVATION DECK. Looking through the BLUE lens, what can you see?

European yellow-tailed scorpion At night, this fierce scorpion uses its big claws to catch prey, such as woodlice. It rarely stings its prey.

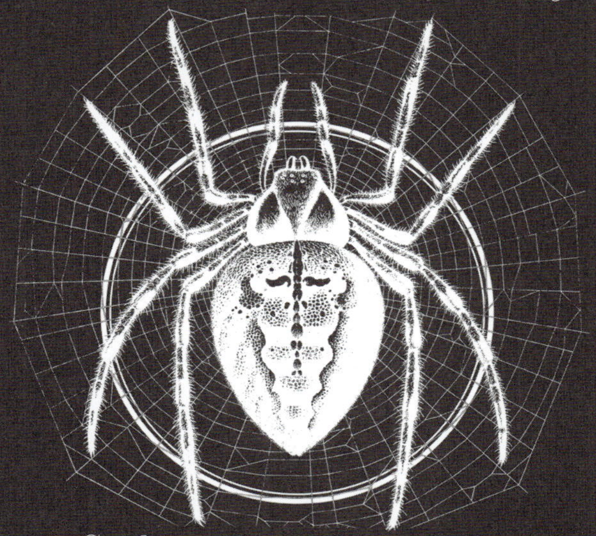

Garden spider The sticky threads of this spider's web trap insects. It injects venom into its victims, wrapping them in silk to stop them moving.

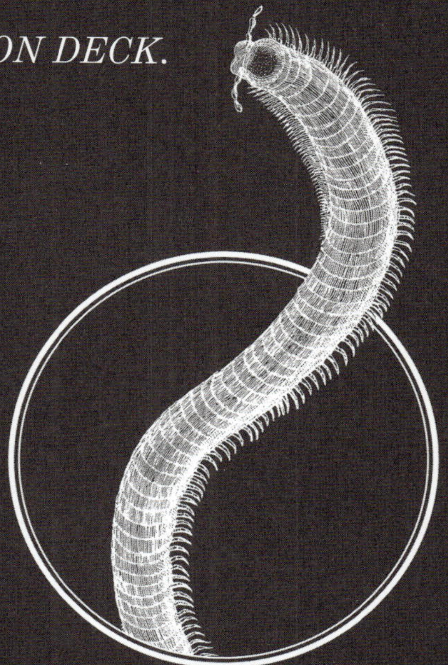

White-legged snake millipede This millipede has about 100 legs, with two pairs on each segment. It eats decaying plants and helps to recycle nutrients.

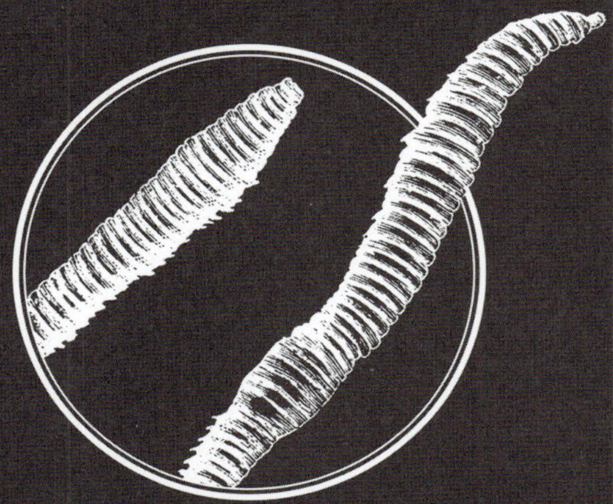

Earthworm Earthworm burrows allow air, water and nutrients to reach deep into the soil. Earthworms grip the soil with tiny bristles.

Nursery web spider Male nursery web spiders present an insect gift to their chosen female. While she feeds, the male can mate with her in safety.

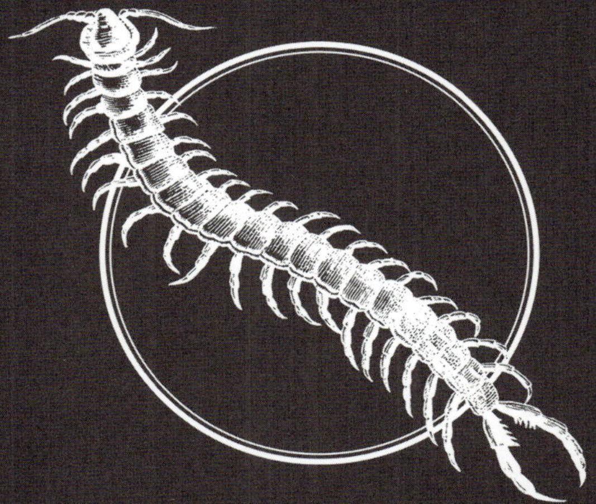

Common centipede As night falls, the common centipede emerges to hunt, sprinting after spiders, slugs, and worms on fifteen pairs of long, spindly legs.

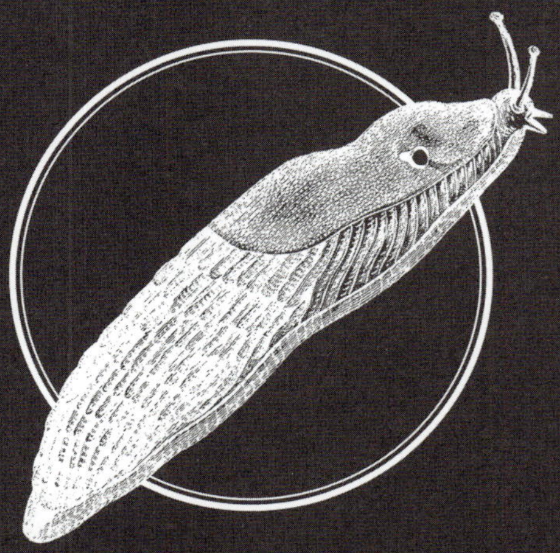

Black slug Covered in a thick mucus, this slug tastes horrible to predators. The mucus also stops its body from drying out and helps it to slide along.

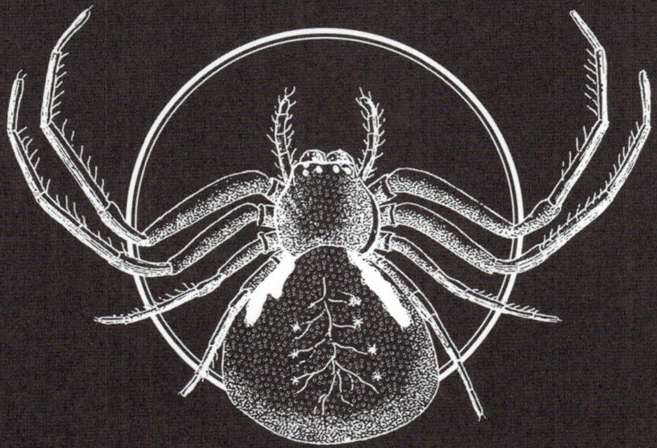

Flower crab spider Female flower crab spiders slowly change color to match the flowers they sit on to wait for prey.

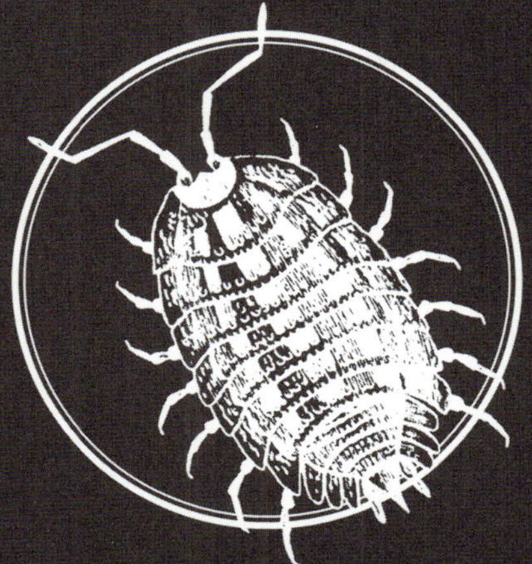

Woodlouse A relative of crabs and shrimps, this hardy minibeast wears a suit of armor to protect itself from predators, such as toads and spiders.

ASIA

From a moth with wings as wide as this page and beetles shaped like violins, to a spider that spits glue and blood-sucking leeches and mosquitoes, Asia is home to some of the largest, most extraordinary and deadly creatures on Earth. It is the largest continent in terms of both area and population. About sixty percent of the world's people live in Asia and insects and other creepy crawlies have to compete with people for living space and food. The range of habitats is enormous, including high mountains, barren deserts, lush rainforests, cold conifer forests and vast cold, dry grasslands. The diversity of species reflects the variety of living spaces, including fifty-seven species of ants in just a few square miles of rainforest in Borneo.

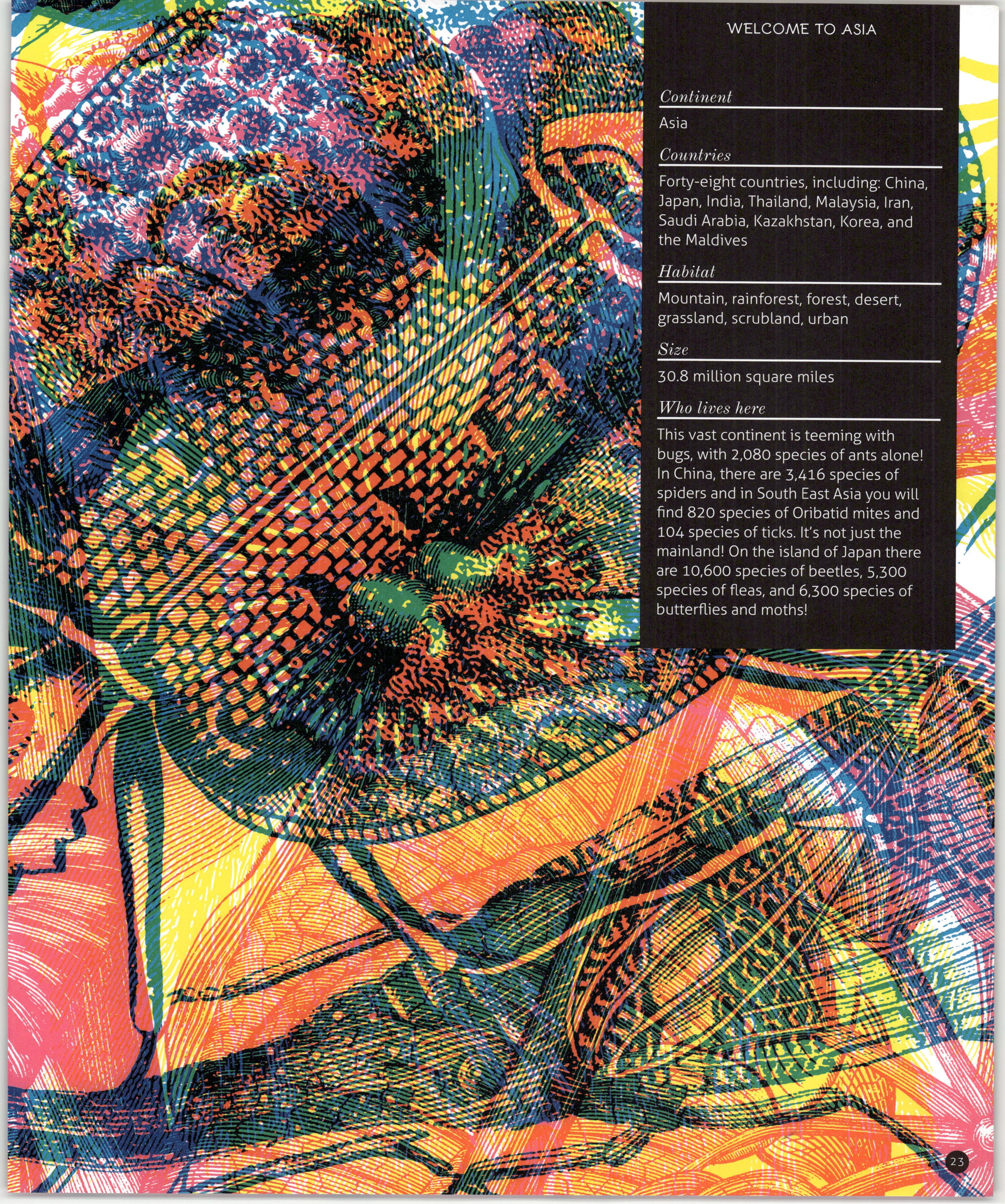

WELCOME TO ASIA

Continent

Asia

Countries

Forty-eight countries, including: China, Japan, India, Thailand, Malaysia, Iran, Saudi Arabia, Kazakhstan, Korea, and the Maldives

Habitat

Mountain, rainforest, forest, desert, grassland, scrubland, urban

Size

30.8 million square miles

Who lives here

This vast continent is teeming with bugs, with 2,080 species of ants alone! In China, there are 3,416 species of spiders and in South East Asia you will find 820 species of Oribatid mites and 104 species of ticks. It's not just the mainland! On the island of Japan there are 10,600 species of beetles, 5,300 species of fleas, and 6,300 species of butterflies and moths!

INSECTS

As dusk falls, an army of hundreds of hungry giant forest ants stirs in the depths of the forest. Gathering at the entrance to their underground nest on the forest floor, they suddenly pour out and scurry up the trees on their nightly sugar patrol. Their goal is high up in the forest canopy—the poop of sap-sucking insects. It is a perfect sugary snack. When their abdomens are full of food, the ant army retreats back underground once more.

READ about the species below and then turn back to THE OBSERVATION DECK. Looking through the RED lens, what can you see?

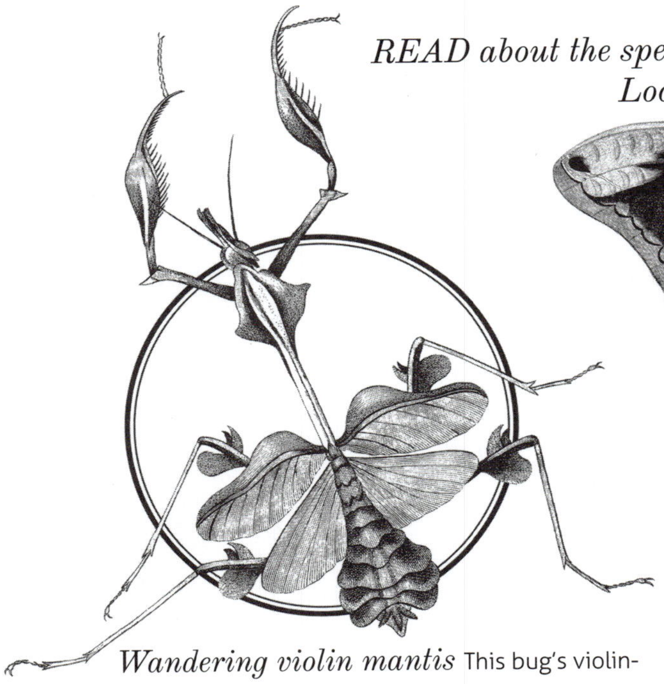

Wandering violin mantis This bug's violin-shaped body is covered in flaps that look like dried leaves, camouflaging it while it waits for prey.

Atlas moth One of the world's largest moths, an adult's wings would just fit across this page! Snake-like markings on its wingtips scare predators away.

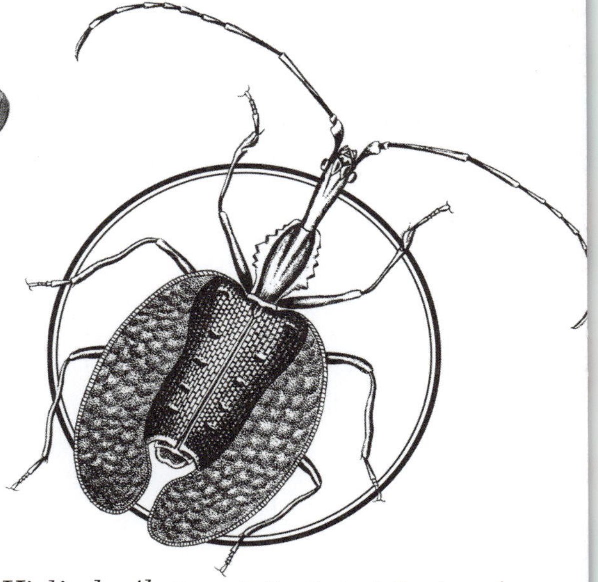

Violin beetle Named after their violin-shaped bodies; violin beetles give off a nasty liquid to protect themselves from predators.

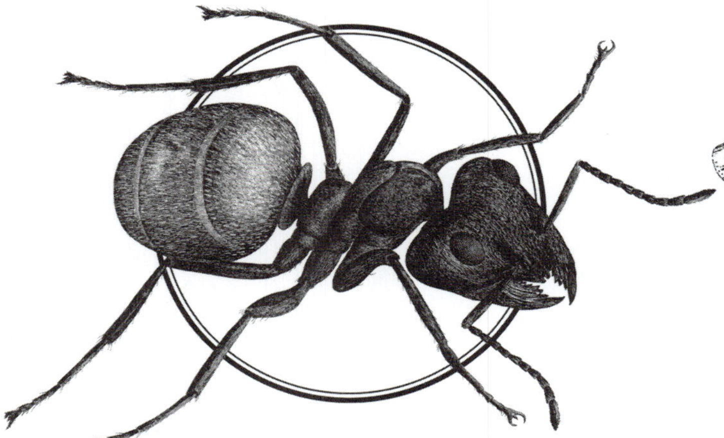

Giant forest ant The largest ant in Asia, the giant forest ant lives in huge colonies of up to 7,000 individuals, with one queen in each colony.

Carpenter bee One of the largest bees in the world, this shiny bee uses its powerful mouthparts to cut nesting tunnels in wood or bamboo stems.

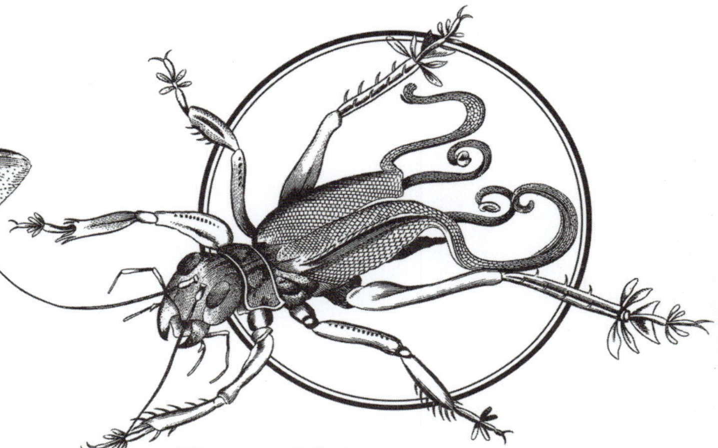

Maize cricket These crickets come out at night. By day, they hide in sandy burrows that they have dug with their strong jaws and spurs on their back legs.

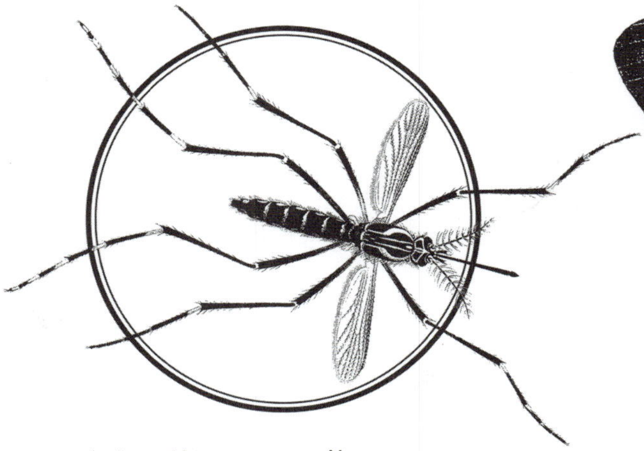

Asian tiger mosquito Female tiger mosquitoes need blood before they can lay an egg. Living for six weeks, they produce more than 300 eggs.

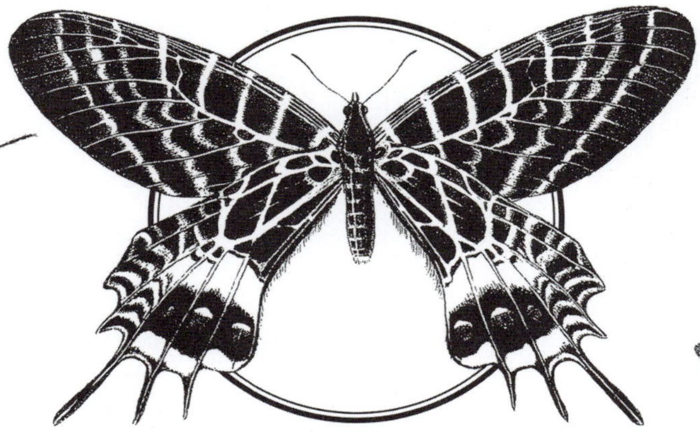

Bhutan glory Fluttering slowly in the shadowy treetops of mountain forests, this superb swallowtail butterfly is hard to see.

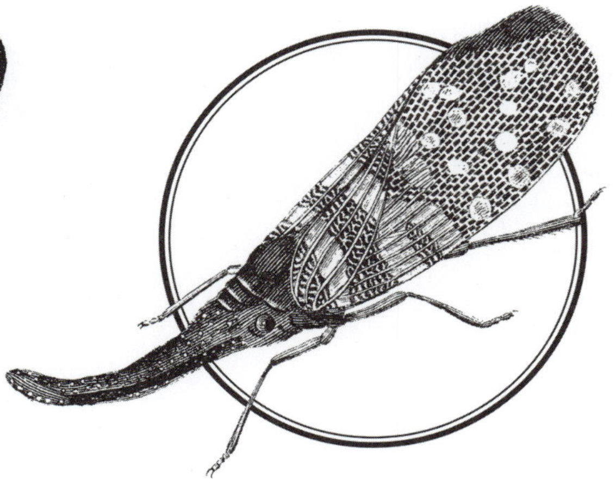

Lantern bug This bug does not give off any light! It uses its needle-like mouthparts to pierce tree bark and sucks the sweet sap flowing underneath.

OTHER CREEPY CRAWLIES

Are dragons alive and well and living in Thailand? Well, perhaps not real dragons, but seriously scary and unbelievable minibeasts called dragon millipedes, which are actually smaller than your little finger. These curious creatures produce a poison in their skin that has stained them bright pink. As well as this poison, they have dragon-like spines on their back to protect them from predators. Dragon millipedes crawl over the forest floor on their many long, spindly legs, feeding on dead and decaying stuff in the leaf litter.

READ about the species below and then turn back to THE OBSERVATION DECK. Looking through the BLUE lens, what can you see?

Thailand earth tiger Living in burrows on the rainforest floor, this spider emerges to catch prey tripping over silk lines at the burrow entrance.

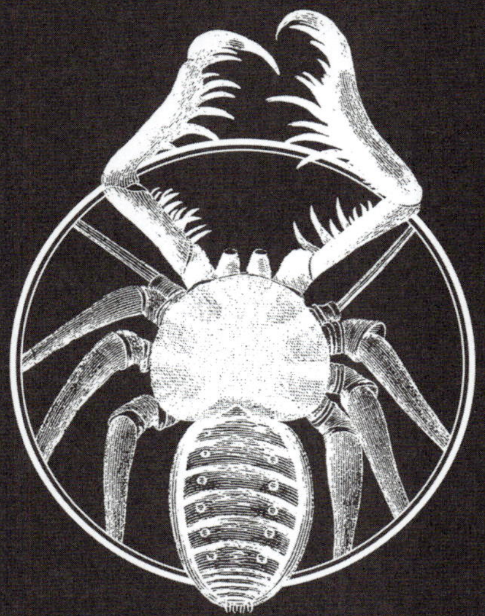

Tailless whip scorpion These well camouflaged spider relatives move sideways and use their strong pincers to hold prey while they feed.

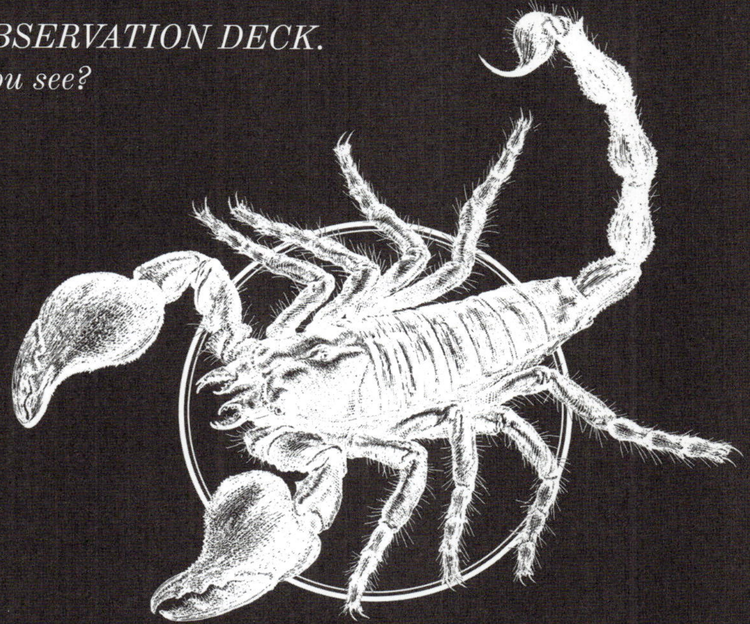

Asian forest scorpion During the day, this scorpion hides away on the rainforest floor and at night it comes out to hunt for insects and spiders.

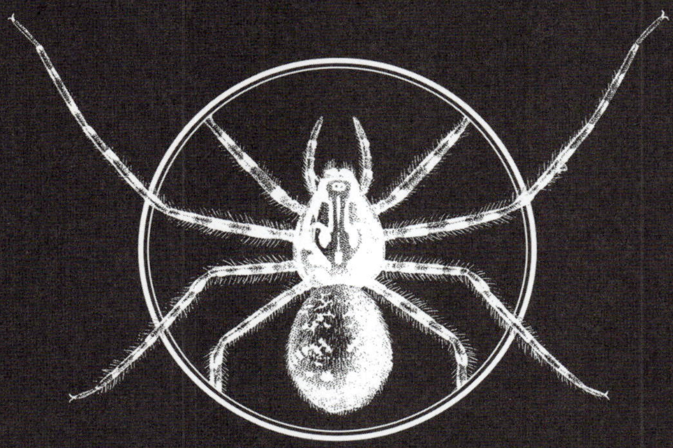

Spitting spider Using zig-zag threads of sticky poison from its fangs, this spitting spider pins down its prey with a net of quick-setting glue.

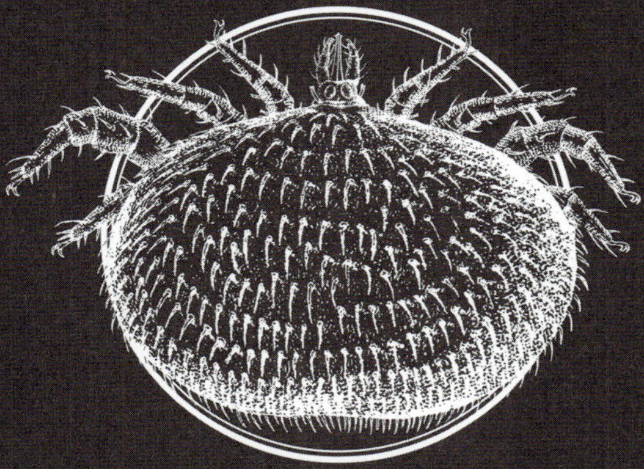

Varroa mite This little mite feeds on the bodies of wild Asian honey bees. It hides away in folds on the bee's abdomen so the bee cannot clean it off.

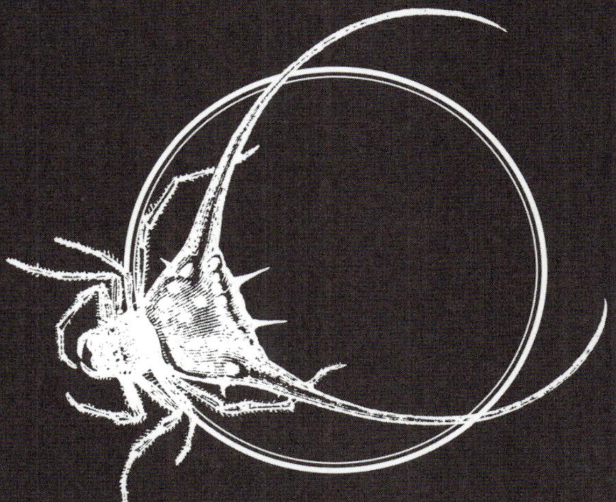

Long-horned orb weaver No-one is sure why these female orb-weaver spiders have such long horns. It may help them to scare predators away.

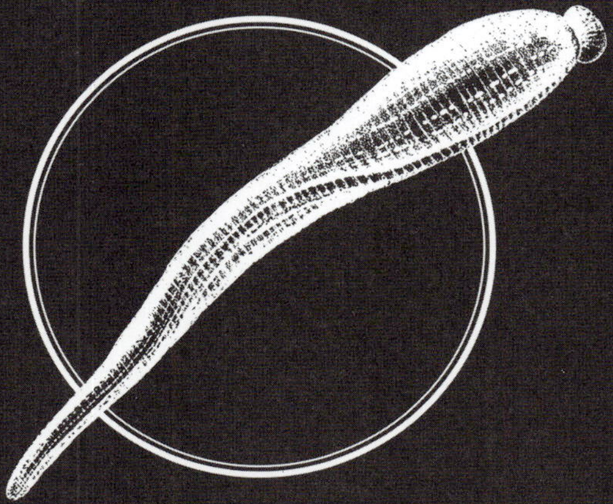

Tiger leech Lurking on leaves in the rainforest, the tiger leech waits for mammals to pass by, then latches onto their skin to suck a meal of blood.

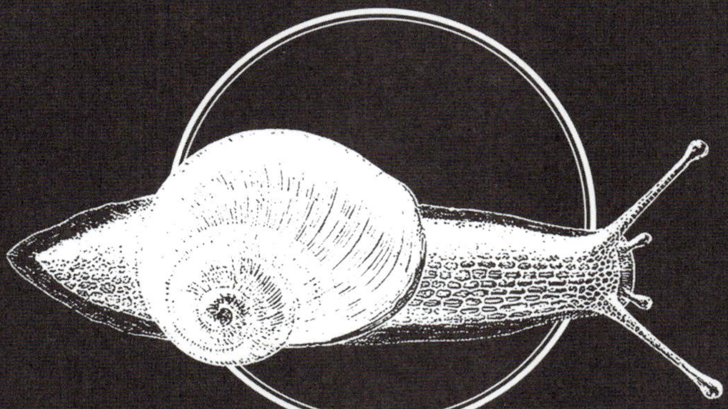

Indian snail This snail lives in the lush evergreen mountain forests of western India. It uses about 100 rows of teeth on its tongue to tear off pieces of fungi.

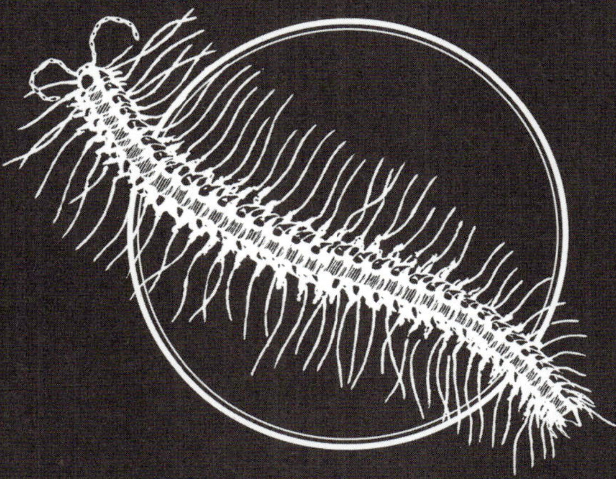

Dragon millipede The shocking pink color of this spiny millipede smells like almonds and warns predators that it is poisonous and they should leave it alone.

AUSTRALASIA

Australasia has been isolated from the rest of the world for millions of years, so is home to many unique bugs. More than ninety percent of New Zealand's insects, including the giant weta, are found nowhere else and many of them cannot fly. Australia is the world's smallest, flattest, and driest continent. Its 200,000 insects and other creepy crawlies, such as desert scorpions, often have to cope with very hot, dry weather, although there are some areas of warm, wet rainforest where a huge variety of species thrive. Rainforests also cover much of the island of New Guinea, the second largest island on the planet, which is home to bird-sized butterflies. Some of the bugs in this part of the world, such as Sydney funnel-web spiders and red triangle slugs, have adapted well to living in towns and cities.

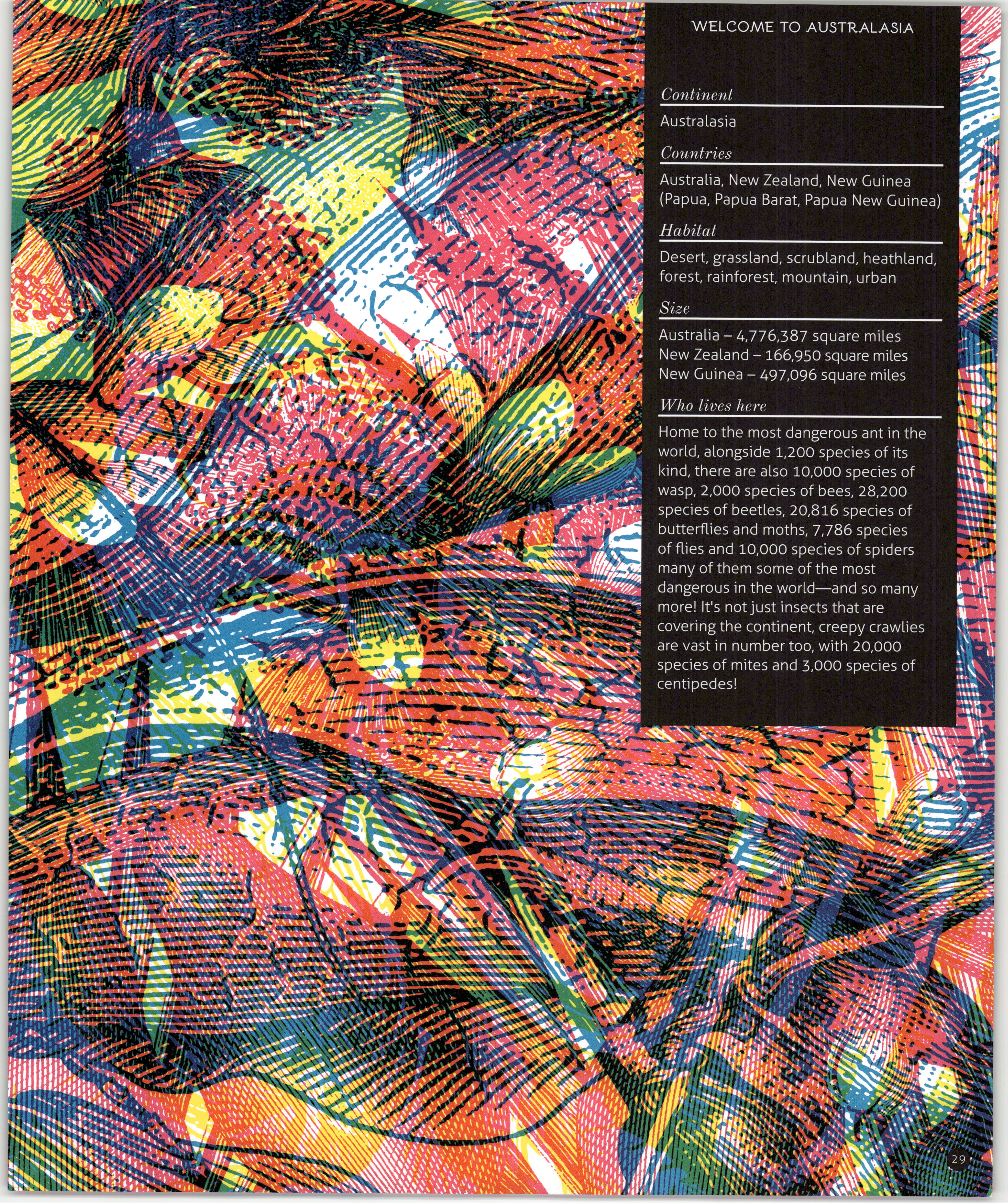

WELCOME TO AUSTRALASIA

Continent

Australasia

Countries

Australia, New Zealand, New Guinea (Papua, Papua Barat, Papua New Guinea)

Habitat

Desert, grassland, scrubland, heathland, forest, rainforest, mountain, urban

Size

Australia – 4,776,387 square miles
New Zealand – 166,950 square miles
New Guinea – 497,096 square miles

Who lives here

Home to the most dangerous ant in the world, alongside 1,200 species of its kind, there are also 10,000 species of wasp, 2,000 species of bees, 28,200 species of beetles, 20,816 species of butterflies and moths, 7,786 species of flies and 10,000 species of spiders many of them some of the most dangerous in the world—and so many more! It's not just insects that are covering the continent, creepy crawlies are vast in number too, with 20,000 species of mites and 3,000 species of centipedes!

INSECTS

Imagine a giant bug whose long, spindly legs will only just fit on a dinner plate... It's the stuff of nightmares! You may be relieved to learn that these wetapunga bugs exist only on islands off the coast of New Zealand and they feed on leaves - phew! They are too heavy to fly but are fantastic runners and jumpers. Over seventy of their cousins also live in New Zealand, including the tree weta, the cave weta, and the Alpine weta, which freezes solid each winter and defrosts itself in spring.

READ about the species below and then turn back to THE OBSERVATION DECK. Looking through the RED lens, what can you see?

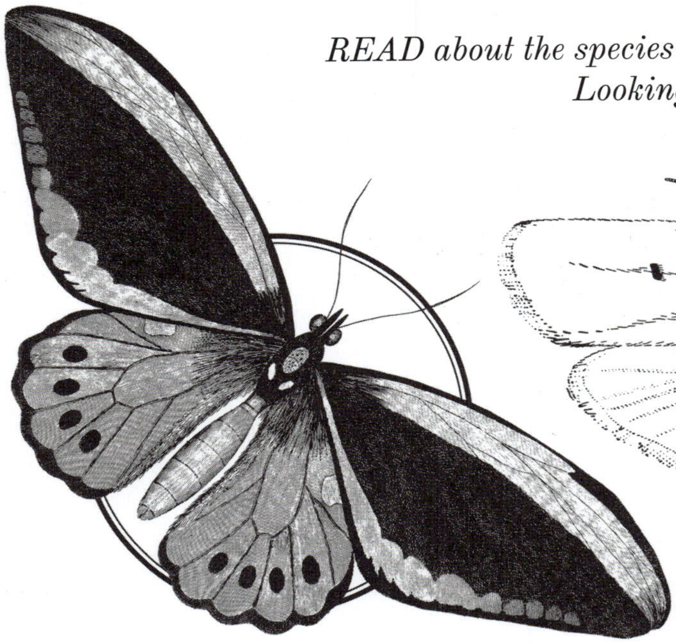

Common green birdwing The electric-green of the male common green birdwing helps him to attract a female. This butterfly is the size of a small bird.

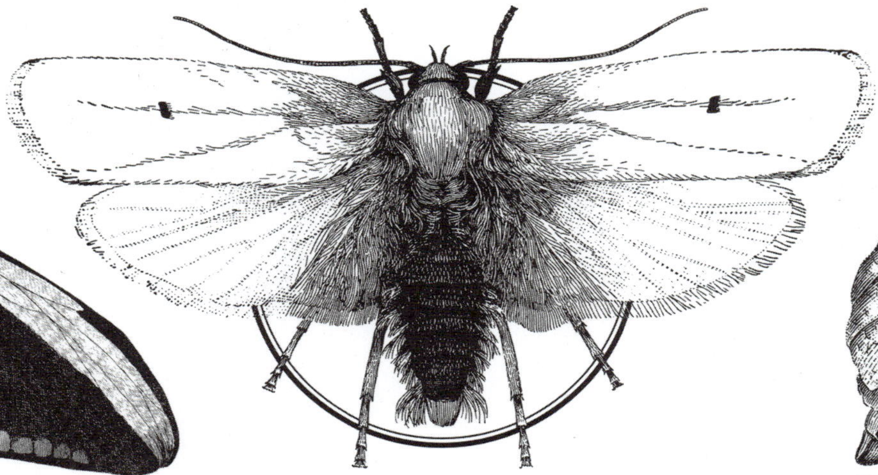

Fruit tree borer When threatened, this moth lies on its back or sides and shows off the yellow tip of its abdomen to scare predators away.

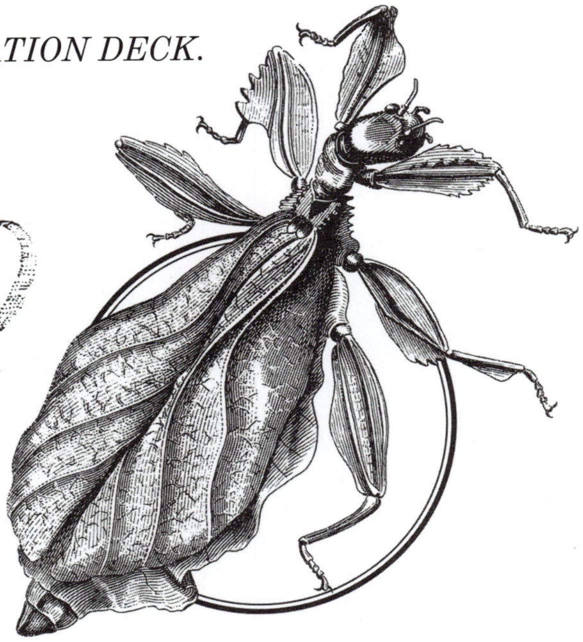

Monteith's leaf insect The female tosses her eggs from trees to forest floor. The nymphs take four months to hatch and then climb back up into the trees.

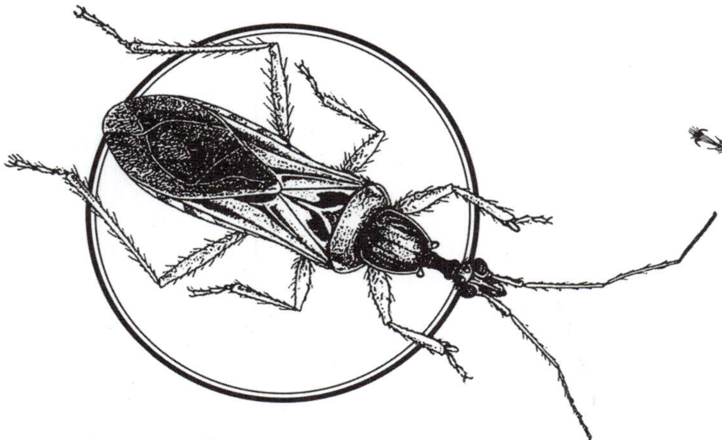

Assassin bug With its sword-like beak, the assassin bug injects poison into its prey. This turns their insides into a mushy soup so the bug can suck its victims dry.

Orange spider wasp The female orange spider wasp provides a paralyzed spider for her grub to feed on when it hatches from its egg.

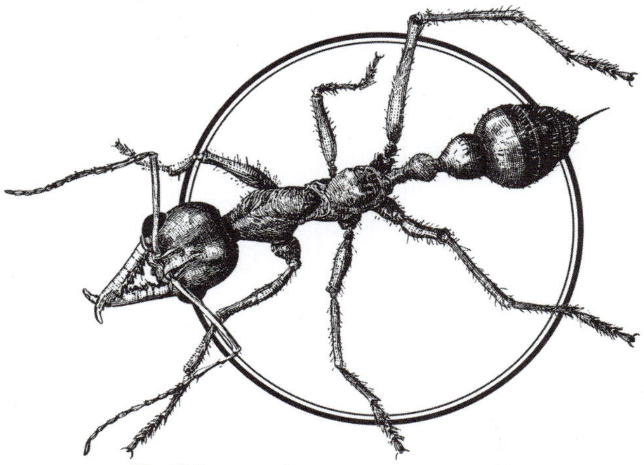

Bulldog ant The world's most dangerous ant, it's named after its savage bite and strong grip. The bulldog ant defends itself with a painful sting.

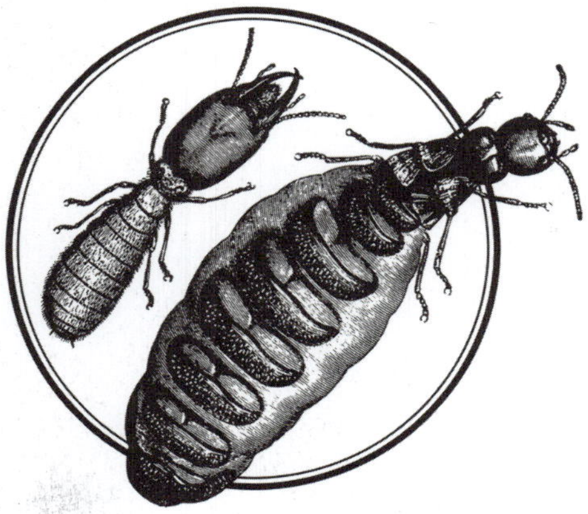

Compass termite Tiny social insects, these termites build huge nest mounds that house up to a million of them, and face north-south like a compass.

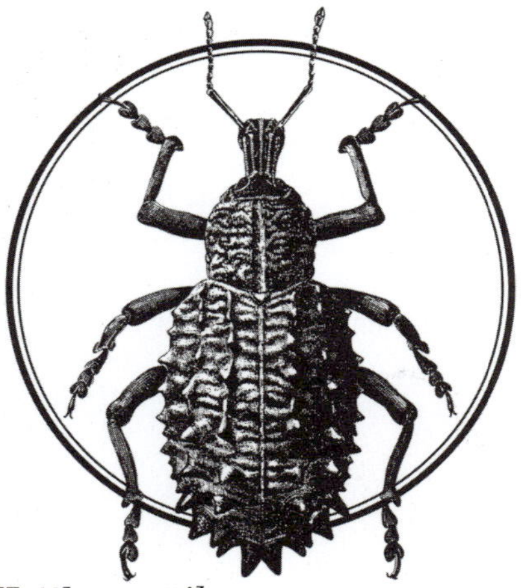

Wattle weevil A type of beetle, the wattle weevil chews on the leaves of plants. Its antennae look like elbows sticking out of its long snout.

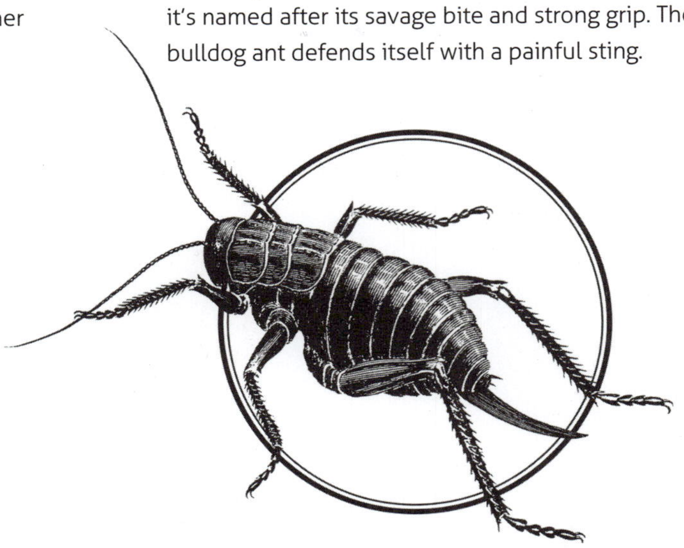

Giant weta Named after the Maori word "Wetapunga", this flightless cricket weighs more than three house mice!

OTHER CREEPY CRAWLIES

During the daytime, the net-casting spider pretends to be a twig, but when it grows dark, this spider puts on its night-vision goggles and sets off to hunt beetles, grasshoppers, ants, and even what it can catch mid-flight! It has more powerful night vision than cats or owls and produces coiled lines of fuzzy silk, which it weaves into a rectangular net to entangle prey. If a net is not used, the spider may hang it over some leaves, ready for the next night, or it may eat the silk. Nothing is wasted in the world of bugs.

READ about the species below and then turn back to THE OBSERVATION DECK. Looking through the BLUE lens, what can you see?

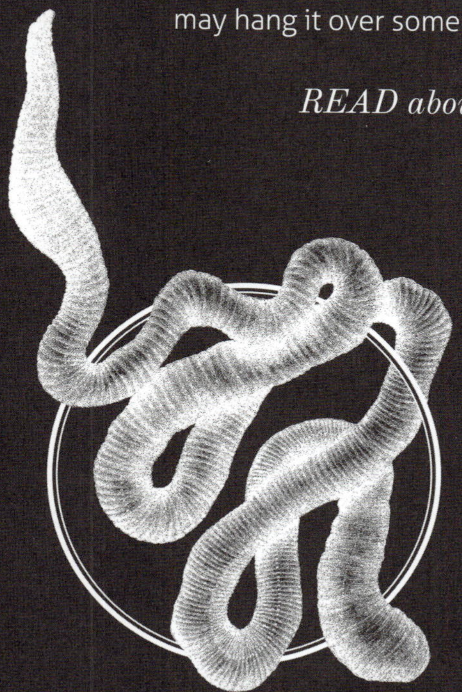

Giant Gippsland earthworm More like a snake than a worm, it makes gurgling sounds as it slides through a network of water-filled burrows.

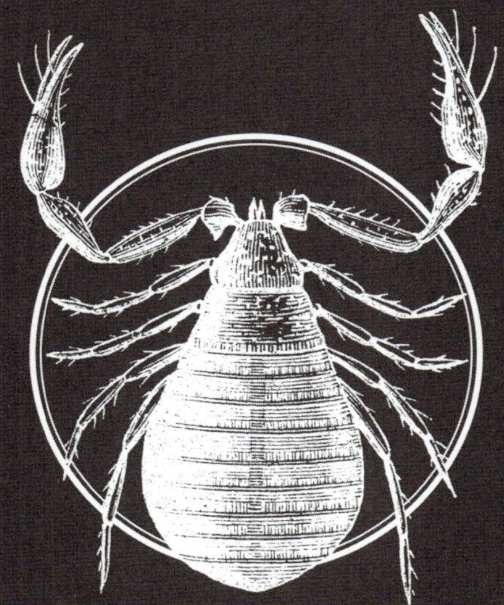

Pseudoscorpion Living only in New Zealand, this tiny relative of spiders and scorpions does not have a stinging tail. It does, however, have poisonous pincers.

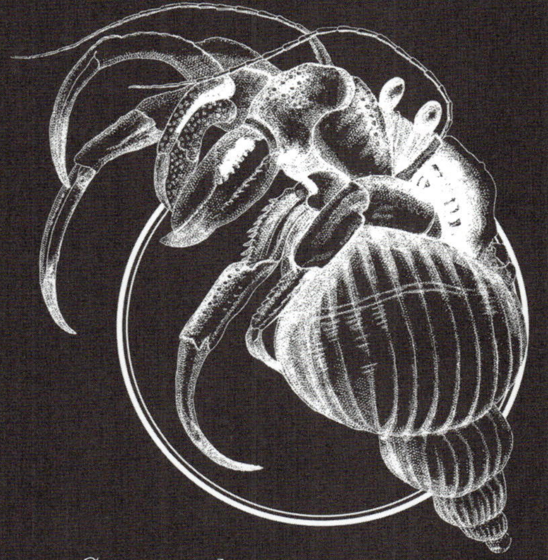

Crazy crab This land hermit crab lives in a borrowed shell to protect the soft part of its body. As it grows, it changes its shell for a bigger one.

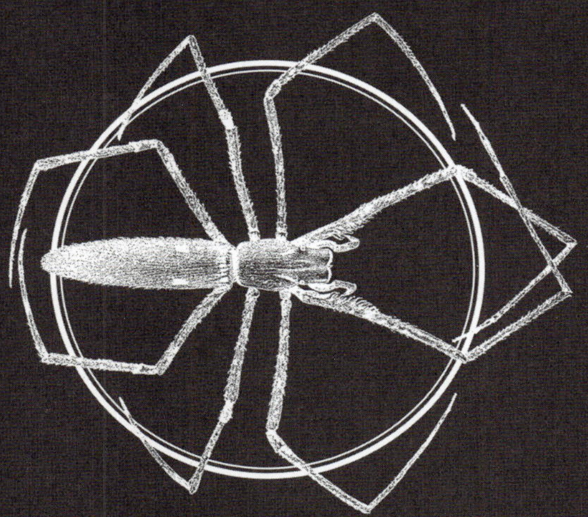

Common net-casting spider At night, this spider spins a silk net to catch prey. It is also called an ogre-faced spider because of its huge eyes.

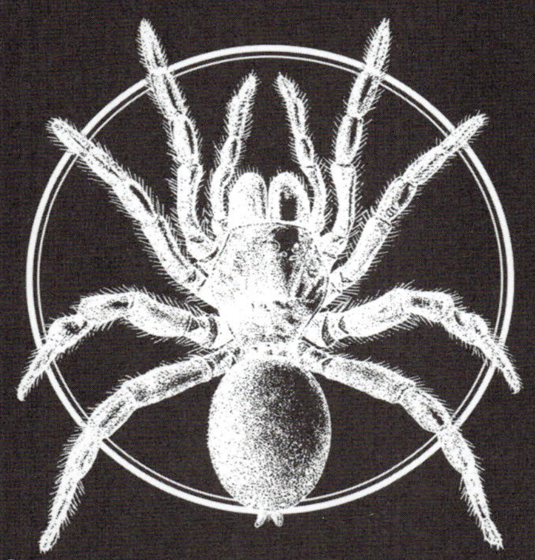

Sydney funnel-web spider One of the world's deadliest spiders, it can kill a person in fifteen minutes. Their fangs can pierce fingernails.

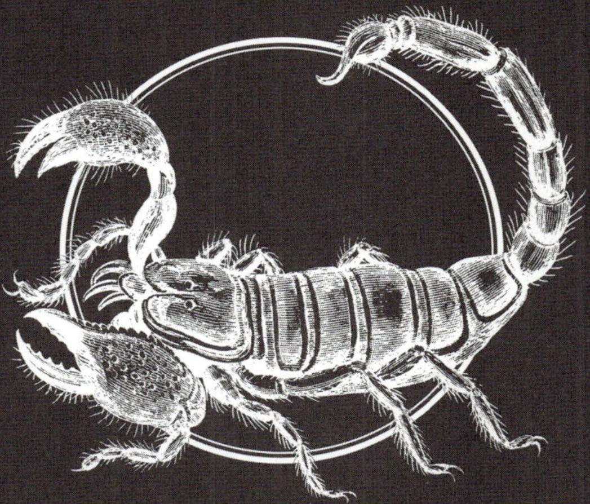

Desert scorpion A robust scorpion, which digs deep burrows with a spiral section. This spiral probably helps to trap moisture in the desert.

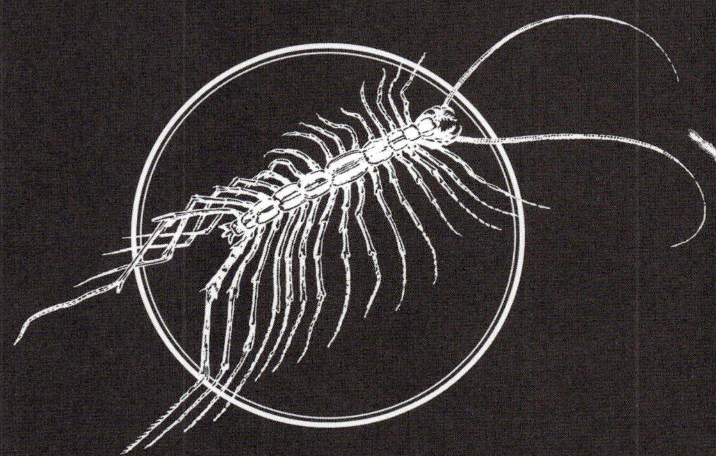

House centipede This centipede runs fast! It traps prey in its long legs and can drop a leg to escape a predator, but the leg will grow back!

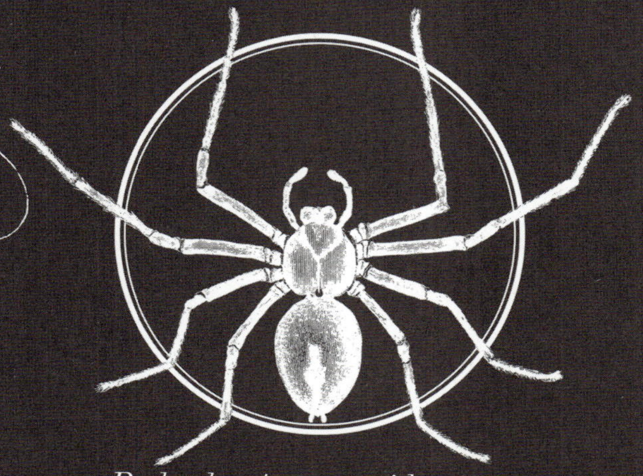

Badge huntsman spider The very flat body of this spider helps it to live under tree bark. It lives in large groups of up to 300 individuals.

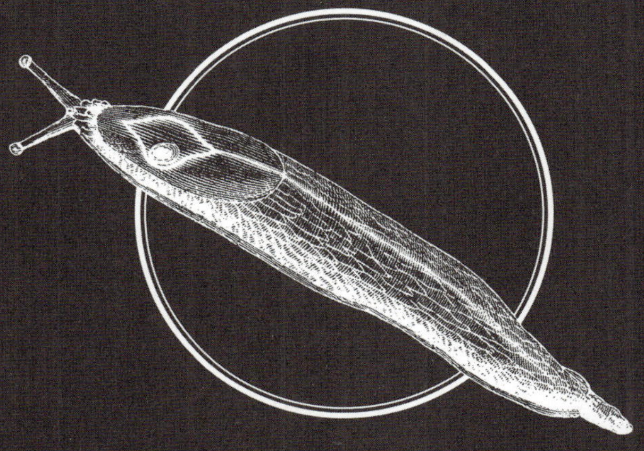

Red triangle slug Australia's largest land slug, the red triangle slug feeds on algae and fungus, even bathroom mould!

CENTRAL & SOUTH AMERICA

South America is a record-breaking continent, which is home to the greatest variety of insects (especially butterflies) and other creepy crawlies on the planet, including the world's longest beetle and the biggest spiders and centipedes. Many of them live in the world's largest rainforest, the Amazon, which provides plenty of food and living spaces. As well as rainforests, habitats in the region include the vast pampas grasslands, the world's driest desert and the snowy Andes mountains—the longest mountain range in the world. South America was cut off from the rest of the world for over sixty million years and most of its insects, spiders, crabs, centipedes, and millipedes are found nowhere else. Today, South America is linked to North America by the land bridge of Central America and people threaten the survival of many minibeasts.

WELCOME TO CENTRAL & SOUTH AMERICA

Continent

South America

Countries

Nineteen countries across Central and South America, including: Guatemala, Costa Rica, Colombia, Chile, Ecuador, and Brazil.

Habitat

Desert, grassland, scrubland, rainforest, forest, wetland, mountain, urban

Size

Central America – 325,461 square miles
South America – 11,085,262 square miles

Who lives here

Ninety percent of the animals in the Amazon rainforest are insects, especially ants, wasps, and bees. There are 2.5 million species of discovered insects in the Amazon, only a tiny fraction of what is believed to exist by scientists.

Bugs do not just exist in the depths of the rainforest! Fluttering around the rest of the continent, as well as many other species, are 3,642 species of butterflies in Colombia, and 3,300 of butterflies in Brazil, that's over 6,000 species of butterflies in two countries alone!

INSECTS

Why would an insect wear a giant peanut on its head? Well, for a start, it isn't a real peanut! From the side, the giant "peanut" on the head of a peanut bug looks more like the scary head of a lizard, or an alligator. It even has a row of tooth-like marks, which might trick predators into thinking it can bite them. Large eyespots on the bug's wings make it look like a big, fierce animal, so that predators leave it alone. This clever bug also has a secret weapon– a stinky spray! However, the peanut bug is not really scary at all - it's just a harmless insect that feeds on plants.

READ about the species below and then turn back to THE OBSERVATION DECK. Looking through the RED lens, what can you see?

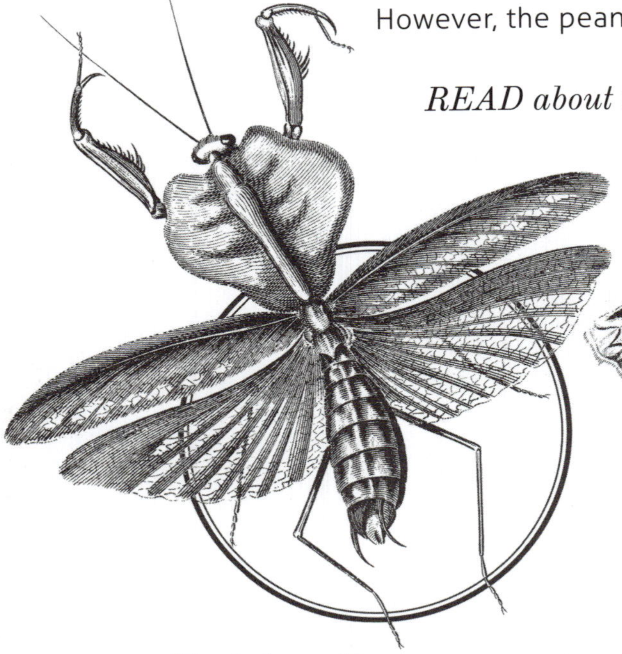

Hooded mantis This praying mantis uses its leaf-like body to hide, then launches a surprise attack on its prey, grabbing its meal with its front legs.

White witch moth Unique zig-zag patterns on this moth help it hide from predators. When its wings are spread wide, it would probably fit along your arm!

Peanut bug Named after the "peanut" shape on top of its head, the peanut bug has straw-like mouthparts that stab into plants and suck up the sugary sap inside.

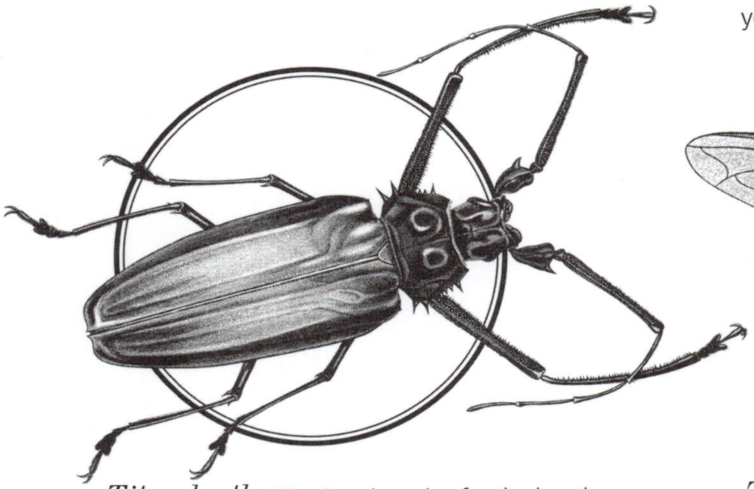

Titan beetle Winning the prize for the beetle with the longest body, this beetle defends itself with jaws strong enough to crunch through a pencil.

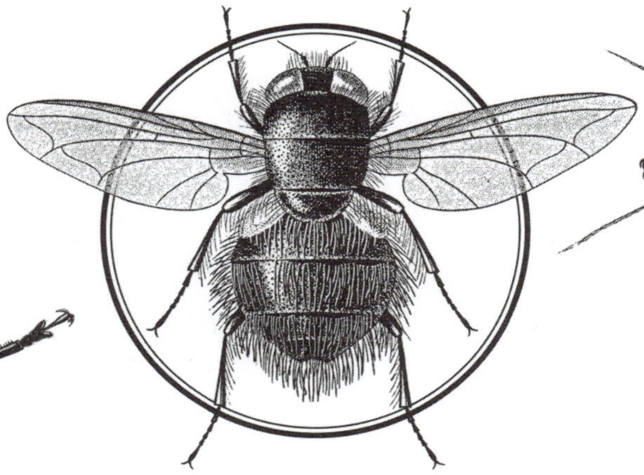

Tachinid fly Living in the tropical forests of the Andes mountains, the grubs of this shiny blue fly are parasites of caterpillars and beetle grubs.

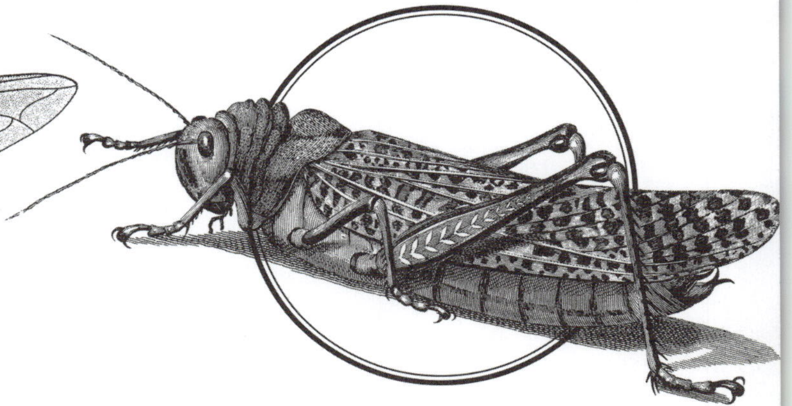

Giant red-winged grasshopper The world's biggest grasshopper, it looks more like a small bird than an insect. Males vibrate their wings to attract females.

Owl butterfly The huge eyespots on the wings of the owl butterfly help it to startle predators, which think they are looking at an owl's face.

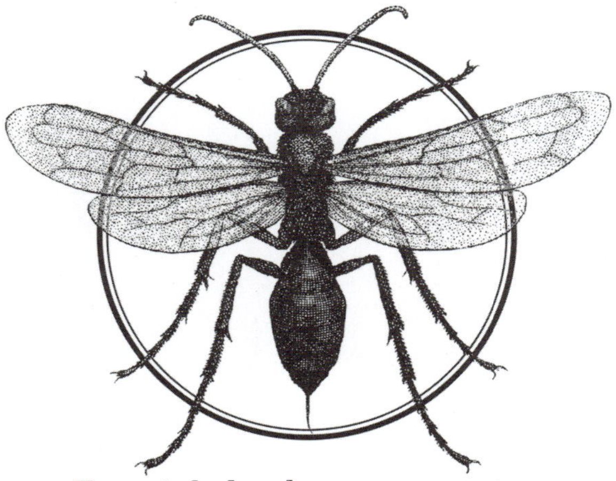

Tarantula hawk wasp After paralyzing a tarantula spider with its powerful sting, the female wasp uses this "living larder" as food for her young.

Bullet ant These ants sting to defend their nest. They have the most painful sting of any insect, thought to be as painful as being shot with a bullet.

OTHER CREEPY CRAWLIES

Creeping through the spooky blackness of the Amazon rainforest at night, a giant centipede sprints across the rainforest floor on its forty-six spindly legs. Using its long antennae to feel its way forward, this eating machine easily overcomes small animals, such as tarantulas, worms, lizards, snakes, birds, and mice. It kills its prey with an injection of fast-acting venom before starting on its night-time snacks. Sometimes, it even climbs into caves, hanging from the walls to grab bats as they fly past its waiting jaws.

READ about the species below and then turn back to THE OBSERVATION DECK. Looking through the BLUE lens, what can you see?

Golden silk spider Sitting in the middle of an enormous golden web, this spider waits for insects, birds and bats to be trapped in the sticky silk.

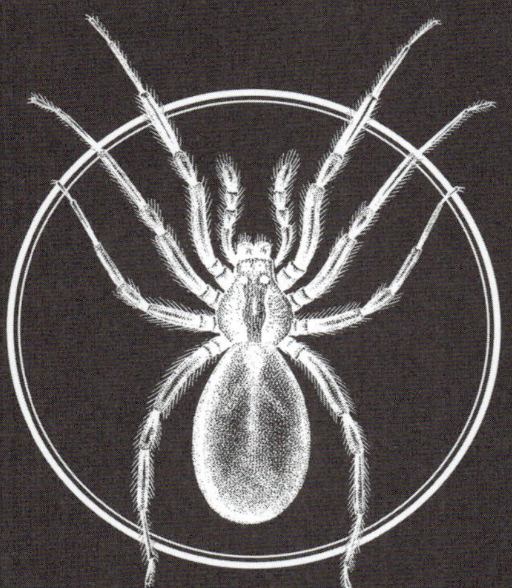

Chilean recluse spider This spider's venom can kill a person. It hides away, surviving for long periods without food or water, and only bites if disturbed.

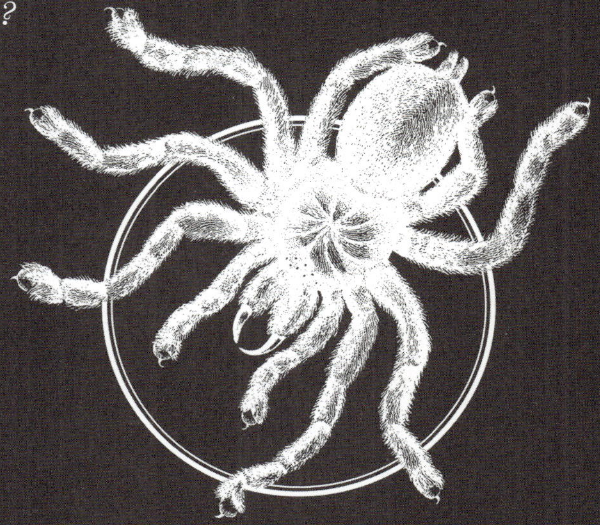

Goliath tarantula The biggest spider in the world, this tarantula flicks barbed hairs at its attackers and is strong enough to catch prey as large as birds.

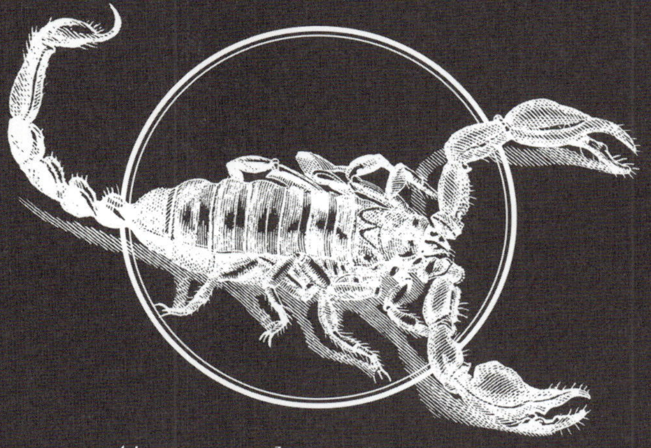

Atacama red scorpion The color of this fast and fierce scorpion helps to camouflage it from both predators and prey as it runs across the desert.

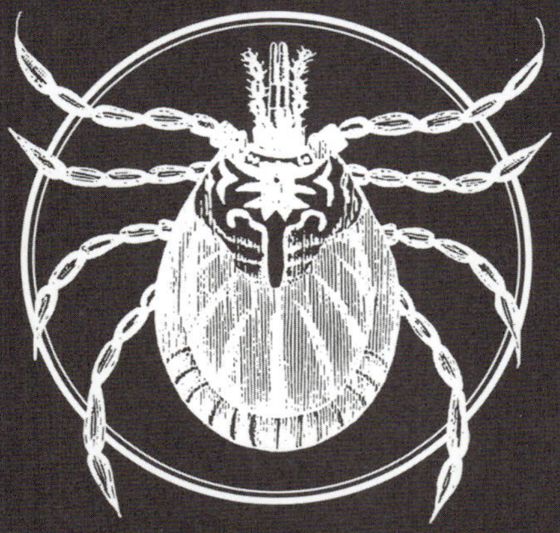

Cayenne tick With its strong mouthparts, this tick clings to animals, such as horses, and uses its saliva to keep the blood flowing while it feeds.

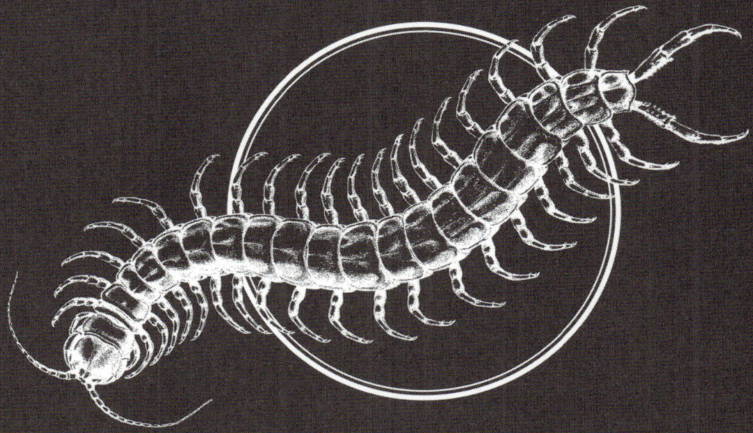

Amazonian giant centipede The biggest centipede, this bug is as long as your arm! Females hold their eggs under their bodies to protect them.

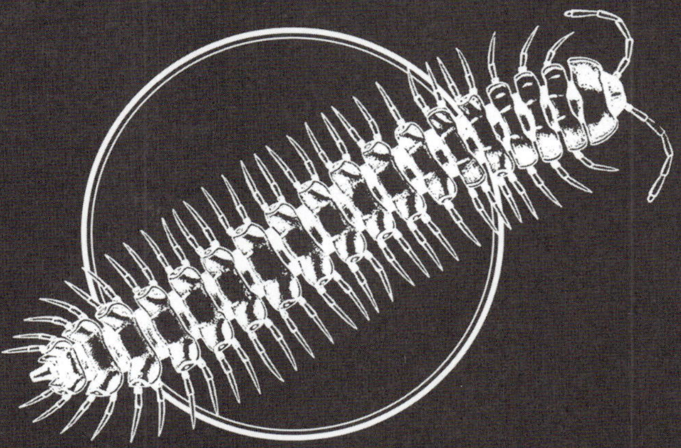

Blue cloud forest millipede The bright blue color of this millipede might warn predators that it is poisonous. It has no eyes, feeling its way with its sensitive antennae.

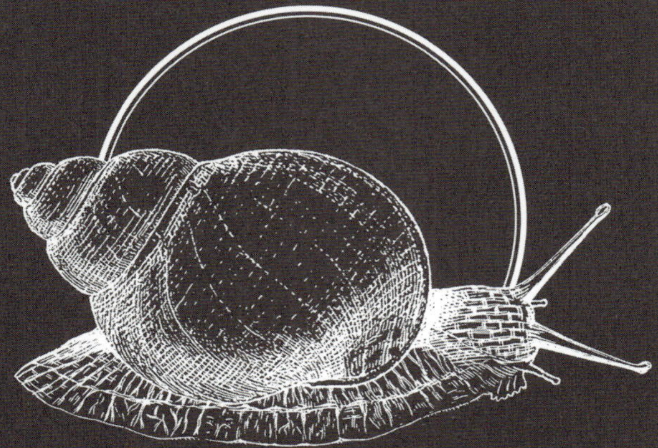

Giant South American snail This rainforest snail has a huge mouth with sensitive flaps, rather like a "mustache", which sense its surroundings.

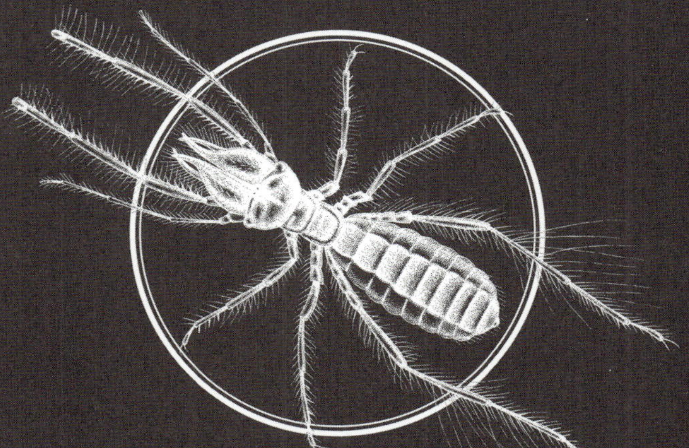

Camel spider This fast-running spider relative comes out of its desert burrow at night to hunt for insects. It uses its big, powerful jaws to catch prey.

AFRICA

A mainly hot, dry continent, Africa is nearly three times as big as Europe and is the world's second largest continent in terms of both area and population. The world's largest desert, the Sahara, covers most of northern Africa. The southern part of Africa has a greater variety of habitats, which range from the rainforests of west Africa and the sweeping grasslands, mountains, and lakes of eastern Africa, to the deserts of southwestern Africa. Many of its creepy crawlies have grown to giant sizes, including the goliath beetle and the giant millipede. Others live together in incredible numbers – colonies of driver ants and swarms of locusts contain millions of individuals. The African continent and the island of Madagascar were cut off from the rest of the world for millions of years, so are home to many unique species, such as the vampire spider and the Madagascar giant swallowtail butterfly.

WELCOME TO AFRICA

Continent

Africa

Countries

Forty-eight countries, including: Egypt, Nigeria, Democratic Republic of Congo, Madagascar, South Africa, Botswana

Habitat

Desert, grassland, scrubland, rainforest, wetland, mountain, urban

Size

Africa – 18,792,750 square miles
Madagascar – 364770 square miles

Who lives here

Amongst thousands of various bug species, Africa is home to over 2,000 species of dung beetles, and probably the heaviest insect in the world! Africa's bugs also include 20,000 species of butterfly, 2,755 species of bees and 760 species of dragonfly. In South Africa there are 6,000 recorded species of wasps, 10,000 species of moths, and over 3,000 species of spiders.

INSECTS

What would you do if a huge, hairy moth with a skull pattern on its back came zooming straight towards you? People used to fear the death's head hawkmoth as a supernatural omen of death and evil. Although this superstition has no basis in fact, scientists don't really know why this moth has such unusual markings. They do know, however, that this moth raids honeybee hives to steal the honey. It cleverly copies the scent of the bees to hide its own scent, which stops the bees from attacking.

READ about the species below and then turn back to THE OBSERVATION DECK. Looking through the RED lens, what can you see?

African death's head hawkmoth If threatened, this moth shows its bright yellow stripes, which make it look like a hornet with a painful sting.

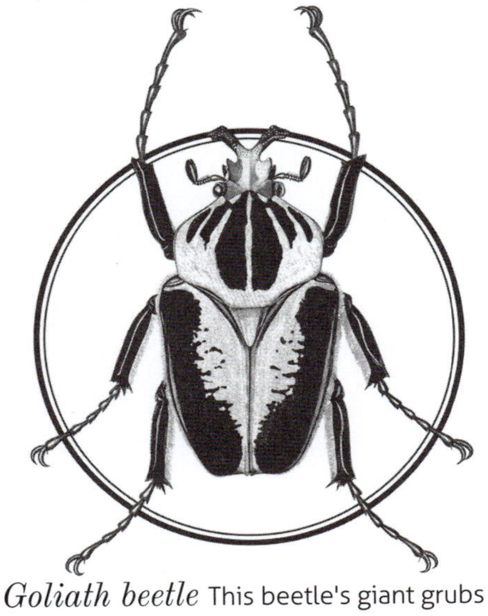

Goliath beetle This beetle's giant grubs are probably the heaviest insect. Adult males have horns, while adult females have a wedge-shaped head for burrowing.

Devil's flower mantis Hiding in plain sight, this mantis looks like the devil's flower orchid on which it sits to wait for its insect prey.

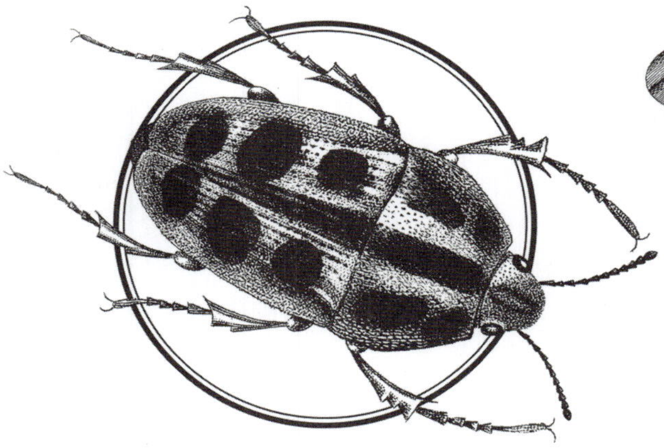

Rainbow shield bug Named after its shiny rainbow colors, this bug is easy to spot. So it produces a stinky smell to keep predators away.

Madagascar giant swallowtail This huge butterfly flies very high and has very long front wings. It lives only on the island of Madagascar.

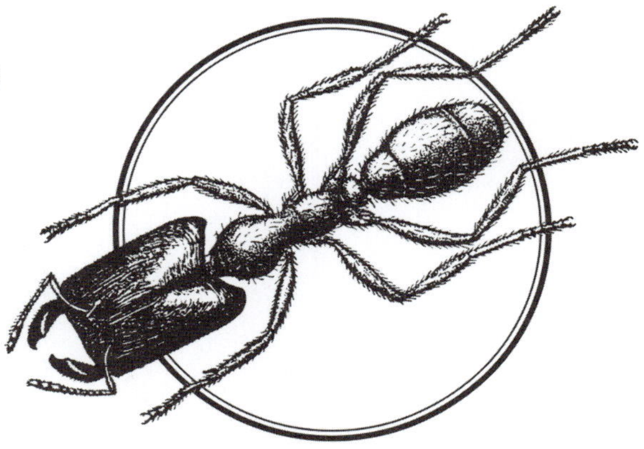

Driver ant Living in colonies of over twenty million individuals, these ants search for food in long columns, using their scissor-like jaws to attack all in their path.

Desert locust This short-horned grasshopper sometimes travels in swarms of billions of insects. One adult eats its own weight in food every day.

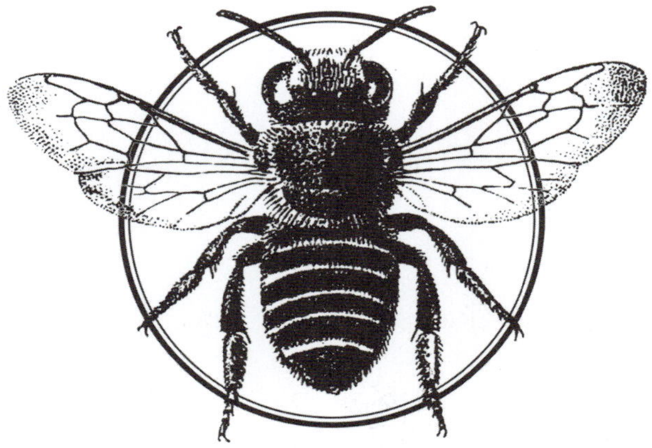

African carder bee Female bees scrape soft fibres from plants with their mouthparts. They use the fibres to make a fluffy nest that looks like a cotton wool ball.

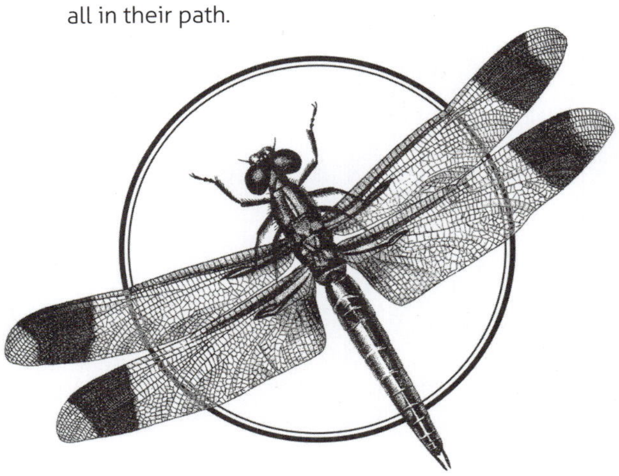

Southern banded groundling This dragonfly is named after the black bands that are seen only on the male's wings, which help him to attract females.

OTHER CREEPY CRAWLIES

If you were walking through the African bush on a moonlit night, a mysterious glow-in-the-dark emperor scorpion might catch your eye. The scorpion absorbs invisible ultraviolet light from the night sky and turns it into a blue-green glow. Scientists have lots of ideas to explain why scorpions are sensitive to moonlight and starlight. It might help them to catch prey, find each other, sense dark hiding places or decide whether to stay on the surface at night.

READ about the species below and then turn back to THE OBSERVATION DECK. Looking through the BLUE lens, what can you see?

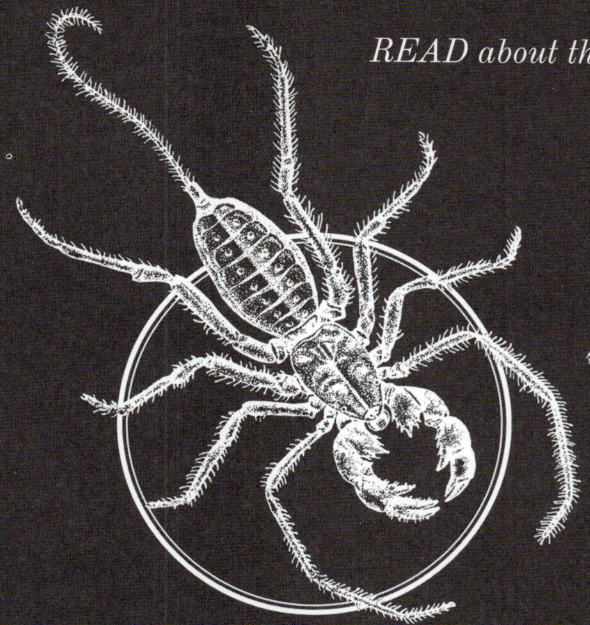

African whip scorpion This harmless spider relative gives off an acidic spray to defend itself. Unlike true scorpions, it has no sting in its tail!

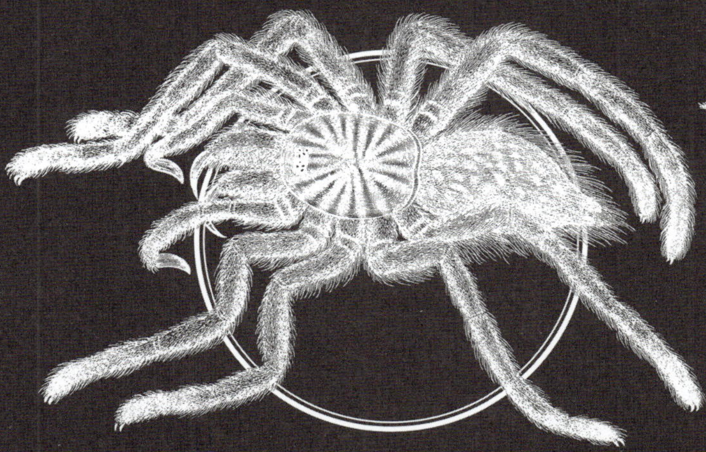

King baboon spider This big tarantula was named after monkeys called baboons because of its hairy body. It has thick back legs for digging burrows.

Common rain spider This harmless spider only just fits on your hand! Females build large egg sacs and guard them for three weeks until the spiderlings hatch.

Giant African snail This tough snail seals itself inside its shell to survive cold and dry weather. It lives for up to ten years.

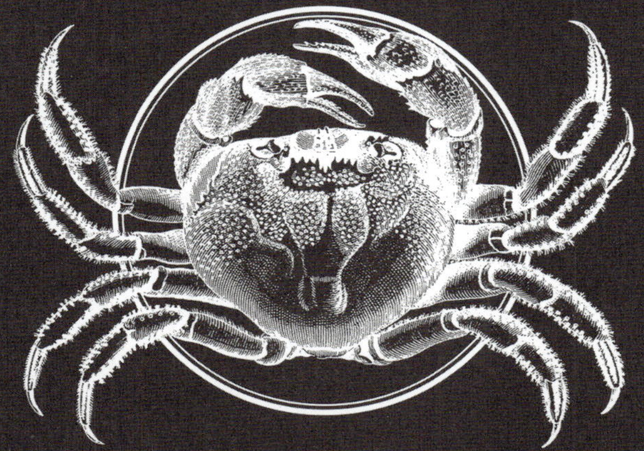

Rainbow crab During the day, this land crab hides out in deep burrows and comes out at night to feed. Females lay their eggs in the ocean.

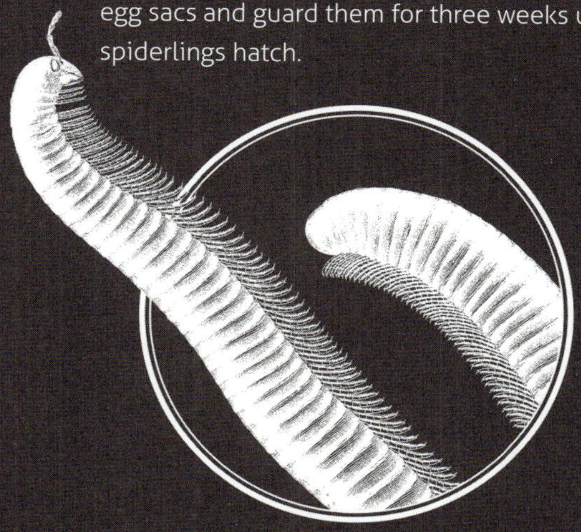

Giant millipede As night falls, this gentle "train" ambles along on its 400 legs in search of dead or decaying food. Its droppings help to enrich the soil.

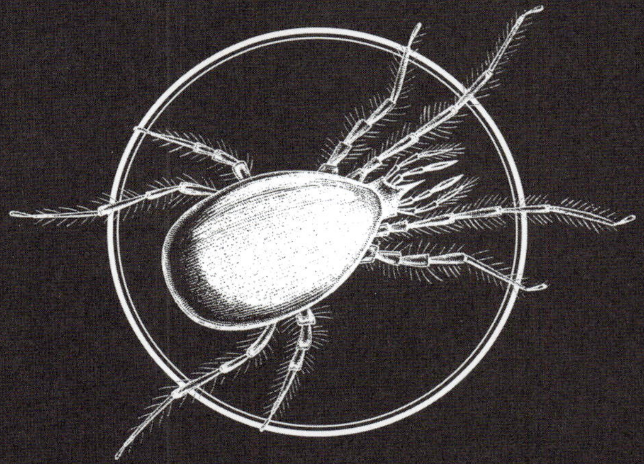

Cockroach mite These mites live on the Madagascan hissing cockroach. Clinging to its legs and around its breathing holes, they share its food.

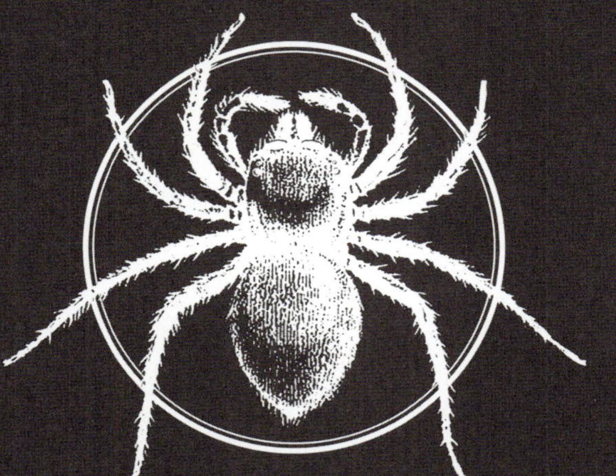

Vampire spider Not a real vampire, but a tiny jumping spider! It feeds on female mosquitoes that have just fed on mammals and are full of blood—yuk!

Emperor scorpion This huge scorpion detects prey via sensory hairs on its pincers and tail. It can survive for up to a year without eating.

ARCTIC

The Arctic consists of the frozen Arctic Ocean around the North Pole and the northern tips of North America, Europe, and Asia. A surprising number of insects and other creepy crawlies manage to live in this harsh habitat, including many kinds of flies and springtails that can survive in frozen soil for several years. Arctic bugs have dark colors to absorb the Sun's warmth, lots of hairs to trap heat and "antifreeze" to stop their bodies freezing solid. Some have very long lifecycles, such as the woolly bear moth, which takes seven years to build up enough energy to develop from a caterpillar into a moth. In the short, cool summers, Arctic bugs spring into action, busily feeding and producing new generations before they are forced to go into a deep sleep (hibernate), or migrate to warmer places as the long, dark winter months draw a frozen curtain over the land.

WELCOME TO THE ARCTIC

Continent

Arctic region: northern edges of North America, Europe, Asia

Countries

Canada, USA, Greenland, Norway, Finland, Sweden, Iceland, and Russia

Habitat

Tundra, snow, ice sheets, glaciers

Size

Arctic Ocean and surrounding land – 9,009,882 square miles

Who lives here

There are over 3,500 species of insects on the Arctic tundra! You can find 1,750 species of flies, 455 species of beetles, 385 species of butterflies, over 300 species of spiders and 425 species of springtails. On the Norwegian island of Svalbard, north of the Arctic Circle, you can find at least eighty-five species of tardigrades (water bears) and 140 species of mites.

INSECTS

As soon as the snow starts to melt in late May, a big bumblebee buzzes noisily among the low-growing Arctic plants as their blossoms unfold. She shivers to generate warmth, which is then trapped by her furry coat. This queen Arctic bumblebee has been sleeping underground for at least nine months, waiting for the ground to warm up. Now she has no time to lose. She feeds on sugary flower nectar to give her the energy to lay lots of eggs. She must build a nest inside mossy mounds and raise two new generations of bumblebees before the brief Arctic summer draws to a close.

READ about the species below and then turn back to THE OBSERVATION DECK. Looking through the RED lens, what can you see?

Arctic woolly bear moth The caterpillars of this moth can withstand temperatures as low as -94°F! They have lots of extra-long hairs to keep them warm.

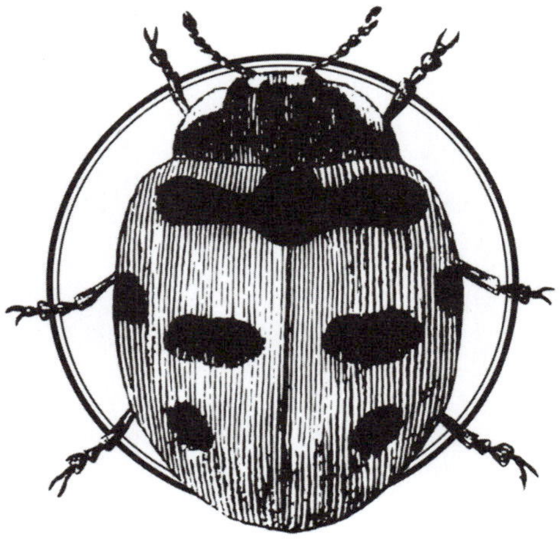

Transverse ladybird This beetle hides away during freezing winters, but in the summer it lays more than 1,000 eggs! It is a predator of aphids (greenfly).

Arctic fritillary The caterpillars of this dark, hairy butterfly hibernate over the long winter months. It takes one or two years for them to develop into adults.

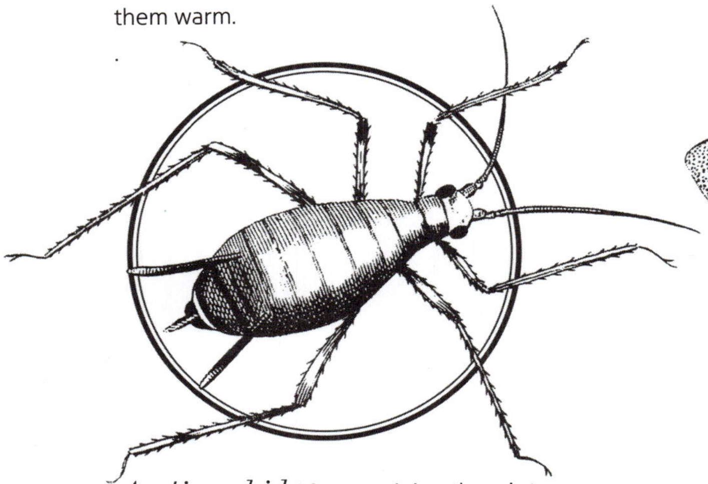

Arctic aphid After surviving the winter as an egg, this greenfly reproduces quickly in the short summer. It feeds on the sugary sap of mountain avens plants.

Arctic bumblebee This big, hairy bee warms up inside bowl-shaped flowers, such as Arctic poppies, which concentrate the Sun's heat, like mirrors.

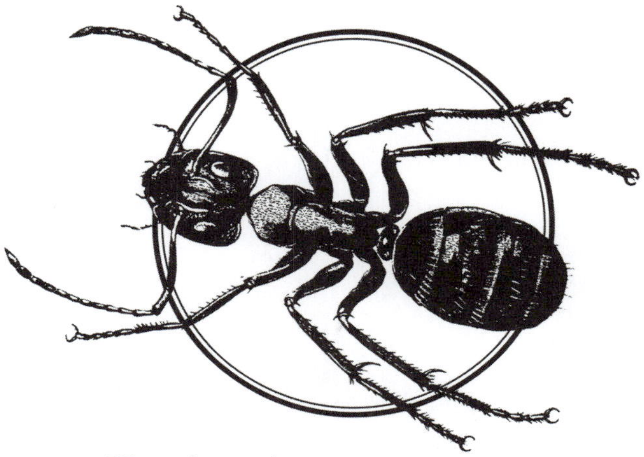

Hercules ant This large ant uses its strong jaws to carve out long nesting tunnels inside the trees in conifer forests on the edge of the Arctic region.

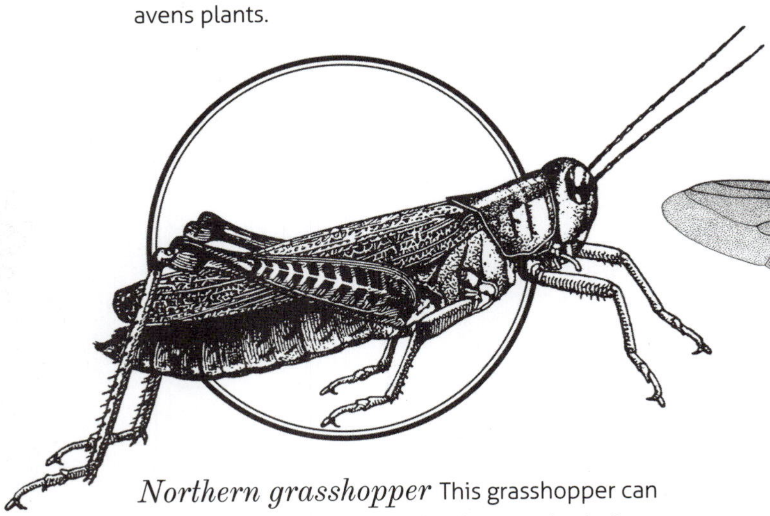

Northern grasshopper This grasshopper can leap twenty times the length of its own body. Its eggs spend two winters in the soil before they hatch.

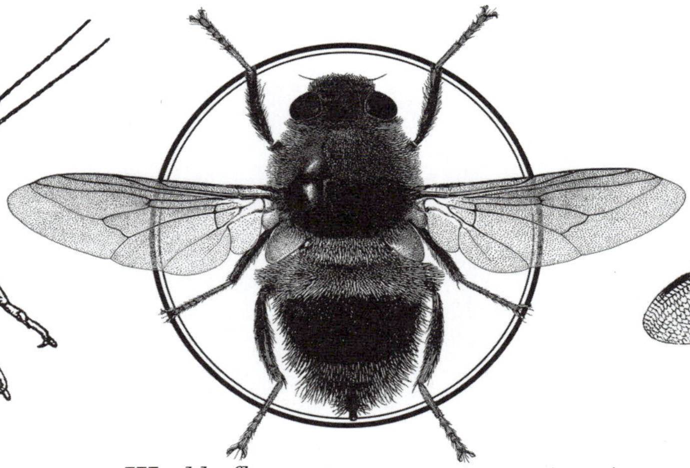

Warble fly This fly's maggots burrow through the flesh of caribou (reindeer). One animal can have 300-1000 of these nasty maggots under its skin!

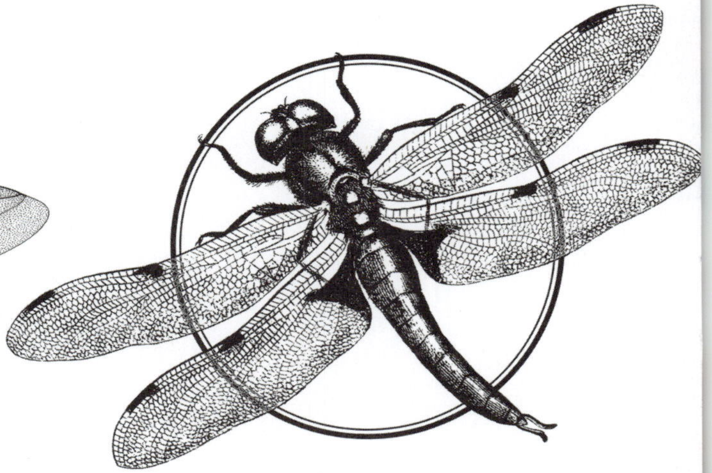

Four-spotted chaser This dragonfly often hovers completely still in mid-air. It hunts for insects over pools and lakes, with females laying their eggs in the water.

OTHER CREEPY CRAWLIES

The icy surface of a glacier does not seem like an ideal place for a bug to live! Yet small, thread-like relatives of the humble earthworm, called ice worms, thrive in the freezing temperatures of this challenging habitat. The ice worm's body contains antifreeze chemicals, which stops it from freezing solid. Its dark color helps to protect it from the Sun's harmful rays but it also burrows deep down into the glacier ice during the daytime to avoid very strong sunlight. Its slim, bendy body helps it to squeeze through tiny holes and cracks in the closely packed crystals of glacier ice.

READ about the species below and then turn back to THE OBSERVATION DECK. Looking through the BLUE lens, what can you see?

Arctic wolf spider This fierce, hairy predator stalks and ambushes its prey on the ground. Its favourite food is springtails, which it paralyzes with poisonous venom.

Ice worm These tough little worms come to the surface of glaciers in the evening and morning to feed on snow algae, bacteria, and pollen grains.

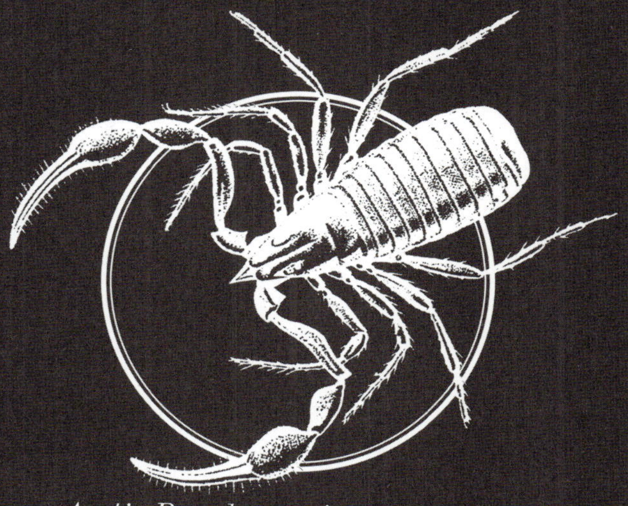

Arctic Pseudoscorpion This pseudoscorpion has pincers like a scorpion, but doesn't have a stinging tail. It does, however, produce silk from its jaws.

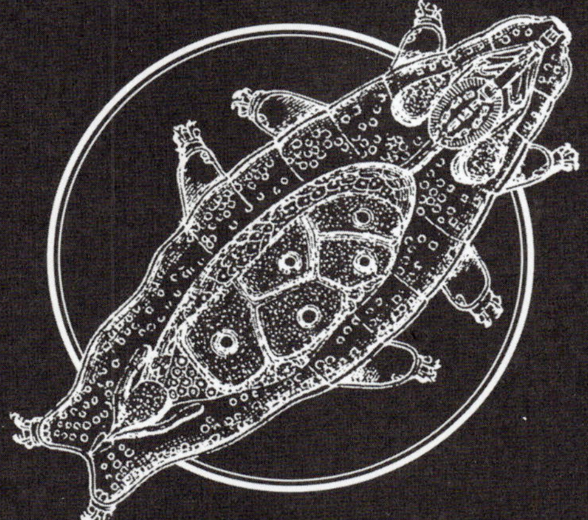

Water bear This tough, microscopic creature survives on glaciers and inside balls of moss, called "glacier mice", which roll over icy surfaces.

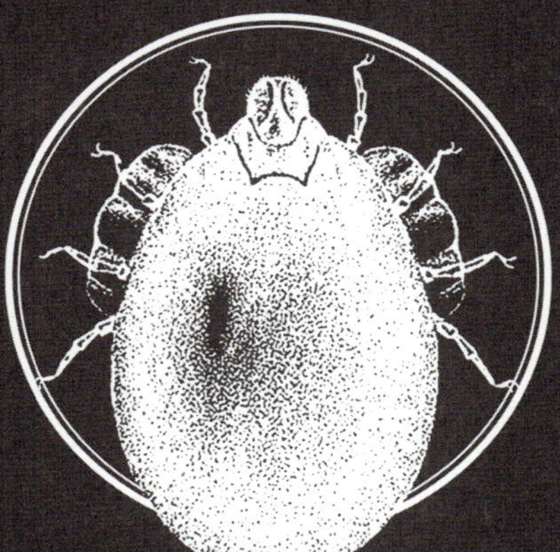

Arctic mite These tiny mites are only one milimeter long! They live in the warmer surface soil and feed mostly on dead plant material, or fungus.

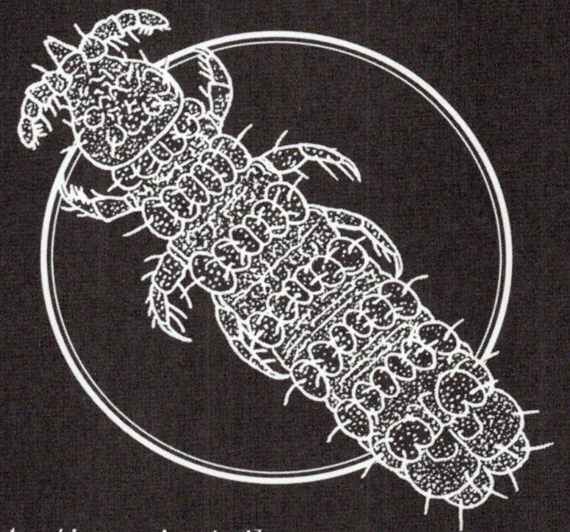

Arctic springtail In winter, this bug dries up so there is no water inside it to freeze into harmful ice. In spring, it soaks up water and comes back to life.

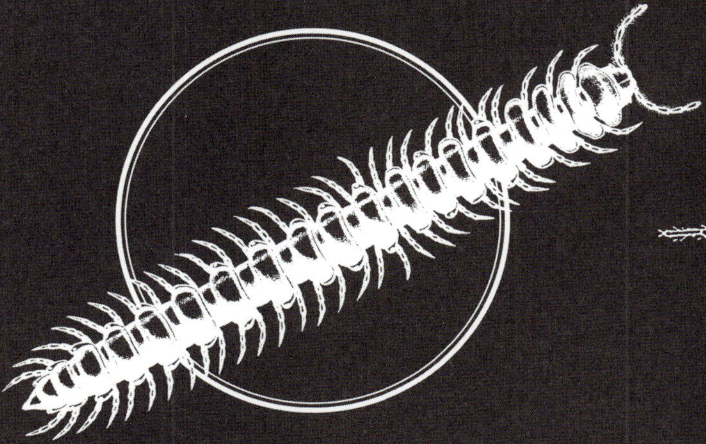

Flat-back millipede These millipedes produce poisonous chemicals for defense and live in the soil. They shelter from the winter as eggs or young.

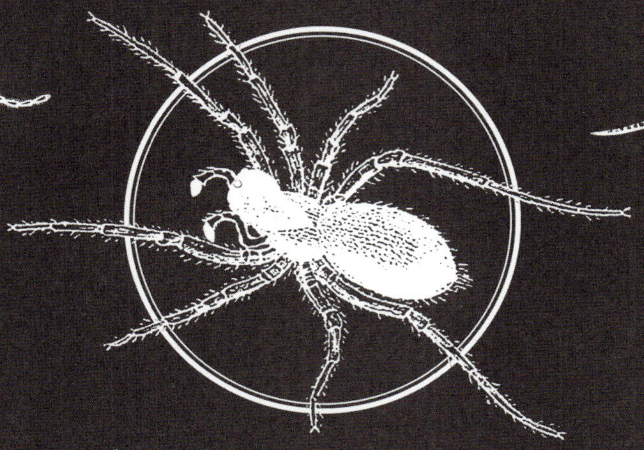

Arctic dwarf weaver This spider floats through the air on its own thin silk threads. It hunts on the ground, or catches its prey in a sheet web of silk.

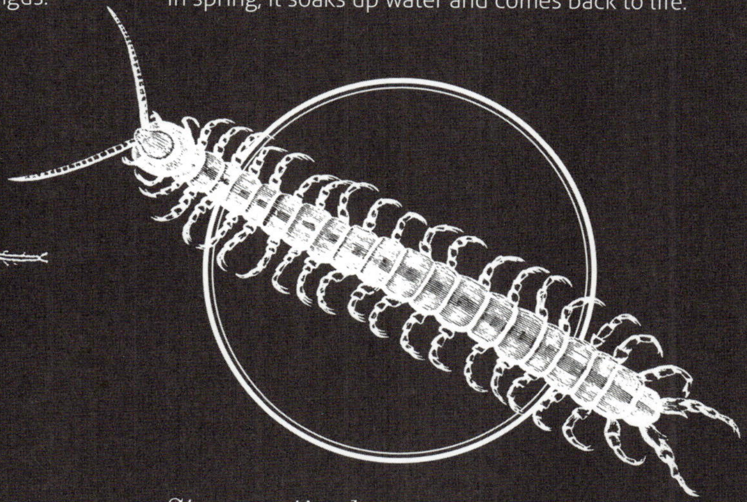

Stone centipede At night, this centipede emerges to hunt for insects and other small creepy crawlies. By day, it hides away in the soil, or under stones.

UNDERWATER BUGS

Only about three percent of the water on our planet is freshwater and most is stored in icecaps and glaciers, or underground. The liquid water in lakes, rivers and wetlands makes up just 0.3 per cent of the world's freshwater. Yet these rare and precious habitats provide food and shelter for up to 200,000 different kinds of insects. Nearly half of all freshwater insects are flies, such as bothersome mosquitoes. Freshwater insects spend one or more stages of their life cycle in the water, with most of them moving onto the land as adults. As well as insects, all sorts of other bugs inhabit freshwater, from crayfish, shrimps, and mussels, to worms and water mites. There is even a spider that spends its whole life underwater! The survival of these bugs is sadly threatened by water pollution and thirty-three percent of freshwater insects are in danger of extinction.

WELCOME TO THE UNDERWATER WORLD

Continent

Worldwide

Countries

Worldwide

Habitat

Lakes, ponds, rivers, streams, springs, canals, wetlands, reservoirs, ditches

Size

Freshwater on Earth's surface (approximately)
Rivers and lakes – 57,849 cubic miles
Rivers alone – 1,317 cubic miles

Who lives here

In the waters of the world there are almost more species of bugs than can be counted. Scientists are constantly discovering new and fascinating insects and creepy crawlies, so the numbers of species are increasing all the time. Discovered so far are a whopping 19,800 species of flies, 6,000 species of diving beetles, 3,000 species of water bugs, 14,290 species of caddisflies, 3,046 species of mayflies, 5,952 species of dragonflies and damselflies, 2,000 species of wheel animals (rotifers) and 5,000 species of water mites.

INSECTS

Did you know that the annoying mosquitoes which whine around your head at night start their lives underwater? Unfortunately for us, most female mosquitoes need to bite and feed on blood so that their eggs will develop. They then lay their eggs on the surface of freshwater. The larvae which hatch from the eggs feed on algae and small water animals. When they are fully grown, they turn into pupae, which float just below the water's surface. Inside a pupa, the larva's body is broken down and rebuilt into an adult mosquito.

READ about the species below and then turn back to THE OBSERVATION DECK. Looking through the RED lens, what can you see?

Great silver water beetle This beetle carries trapped air in hairs under its abdomen. They look like silvery bubbles, and mean it can breathe underwater.

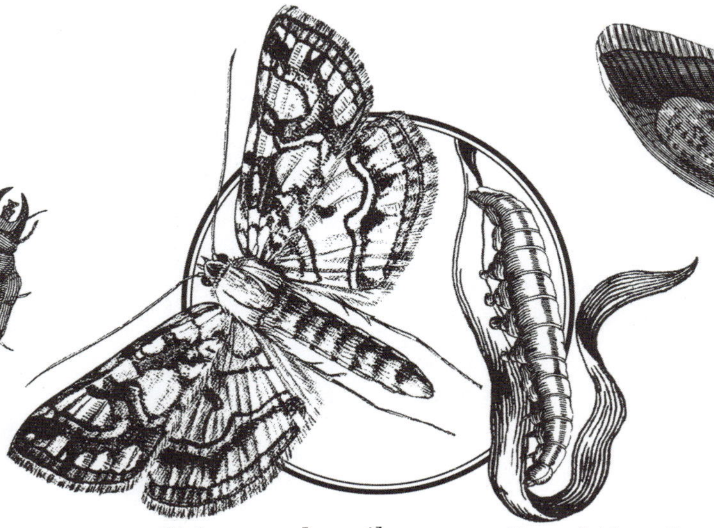

China mark moth The caterpillars of this moth live underwater in an air-filled pouch of leaves bound together with silk threads. They feed on water plants.

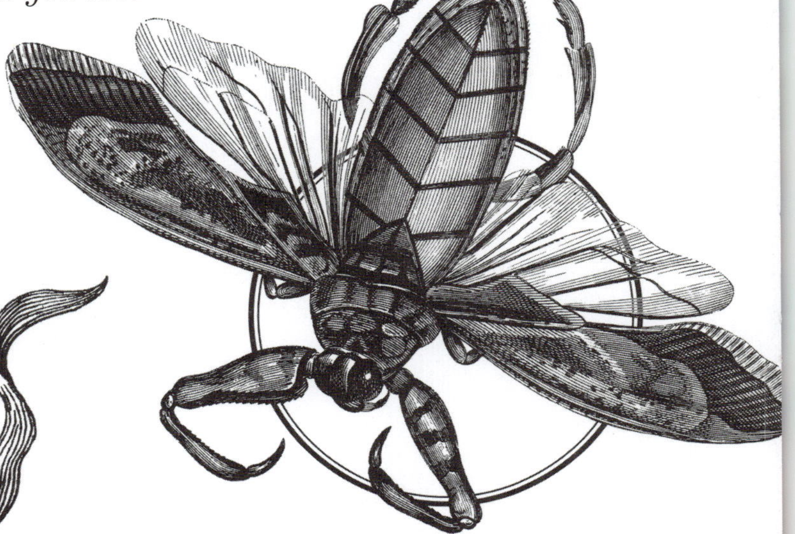

Giant water bug Breathing air through a snorkel on its rear end, this bug uses its hooked front legs to grab prey as big as fish or baby turtles.

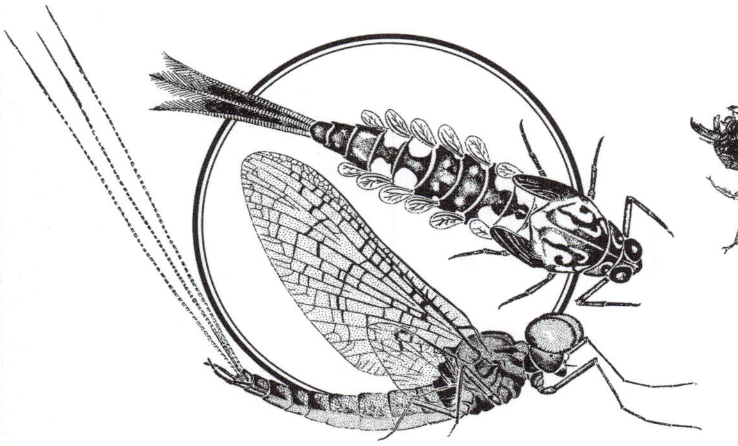

Mayfly The nymphs of mayflies live underwater, using feathery gills to take in oxygen from the water. They graze on algae, decaying matter, and weeds.

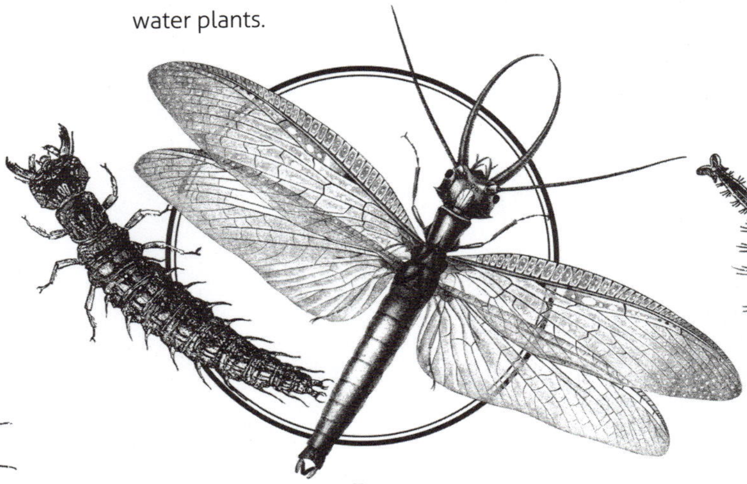

Eastern dobsonfly Adults use their horn-like mouthparts to fight rival males or impress females. Grubs can breathe both in and out of water.

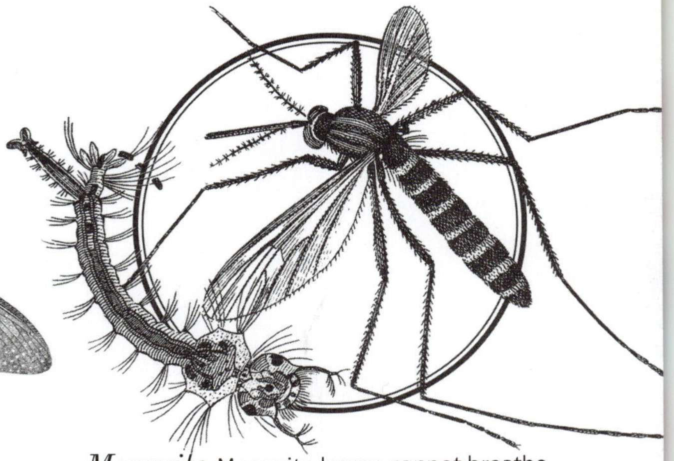

Mosquito Mosquito larvae cannot breathe underwater. They hang from the surface and breathe through a "snorkel" tube at the end of their bodies.

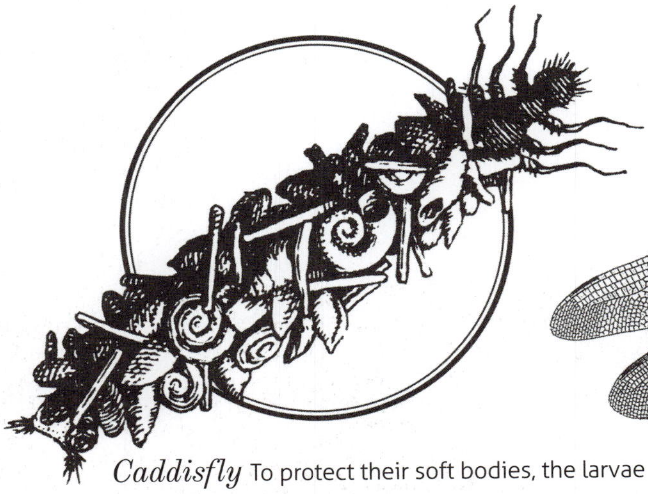

Caddisfly To protect their soft bodies, the larvae build a case of stones or shells. They live inside until they turn into winged adults, which live on land and in the air.

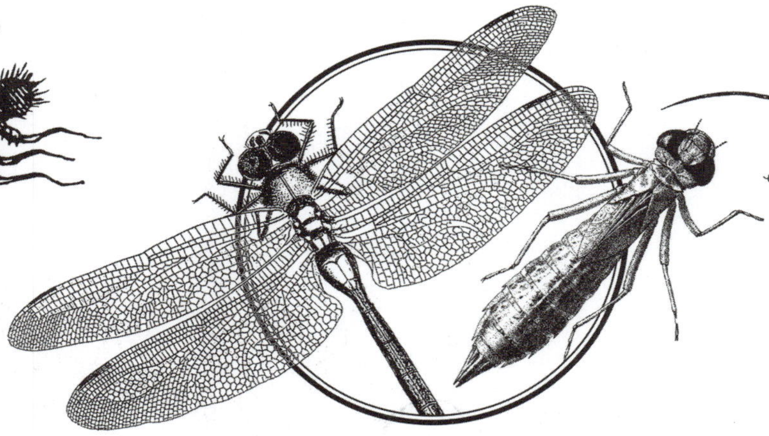

Green darner dragonfly Adults and nymphs are both fierce hunters. Adults catch flying insects, while nymphs feast on water insects, tadpoles, and small fish.

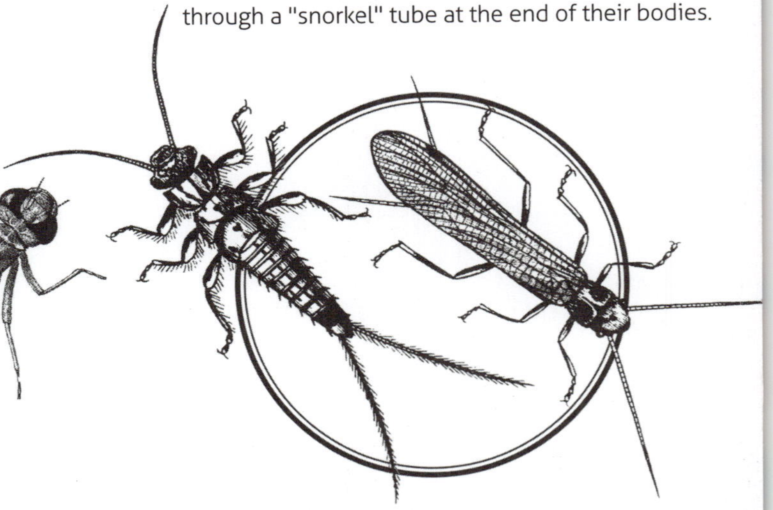

Stonefly The nymphs of stoneflies live on, or near, stones in streams and rivers. When they are ready to turn into adults, they crawl out of the water.

OTHER CREEPY CRAWLIES

Which spider is clever enough to make its own diving equipment? Like us, the water spider cannot breathe underwater, but it can trap bubbles of air on its hairy body and legs. This makes it look as if it is wearing a shiny, silver diving suit. The water spider stores the air bubbles inside its underwater home, which it spins from silk and anchors to water plants. The spider only leaves its air-filled retreat to collect more air, or catch food – baby water spiders are even born underwater!

READ about the species below and then turn back to THE OBSERVATION DECK. Looking through the BLUE lens, what can you see?

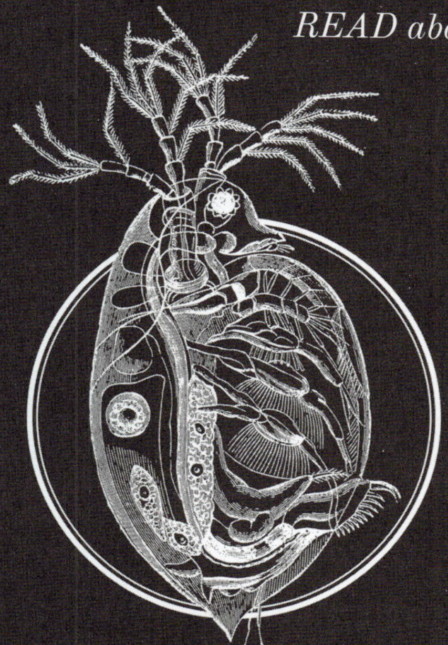

Water flea Swimming in a jerky, hopping way, like a land flea jumping, water fleas use their legs to collect microscopic particles of food from the water.

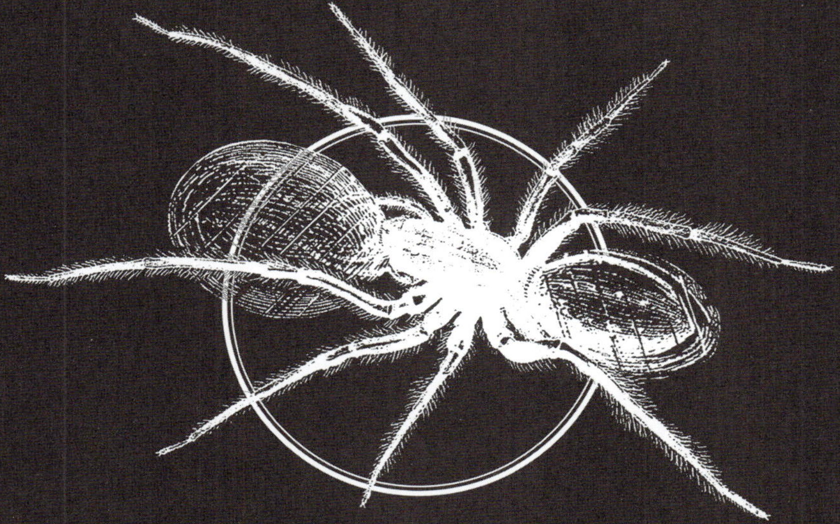

Water spider The water spider lives inside an underwater "diving bell", which it makes from silk and fills with air from the water's surface.

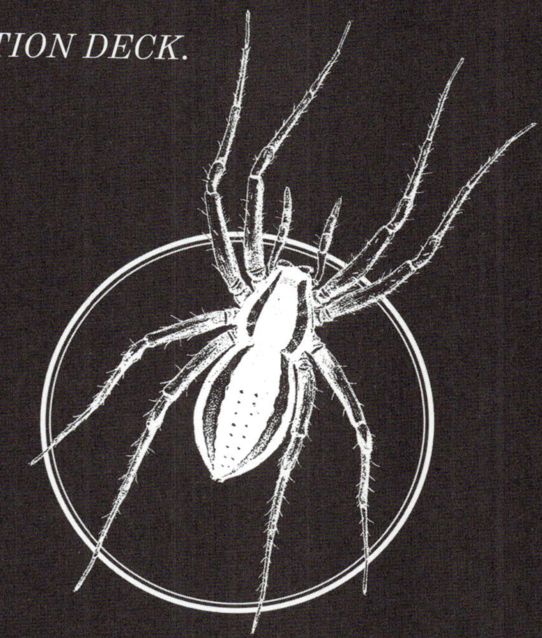

Raft spider This spider floats on the water, feeling the vibrations of prey with the sensitive hairs on its legs. If threatened, it will swim underwater.

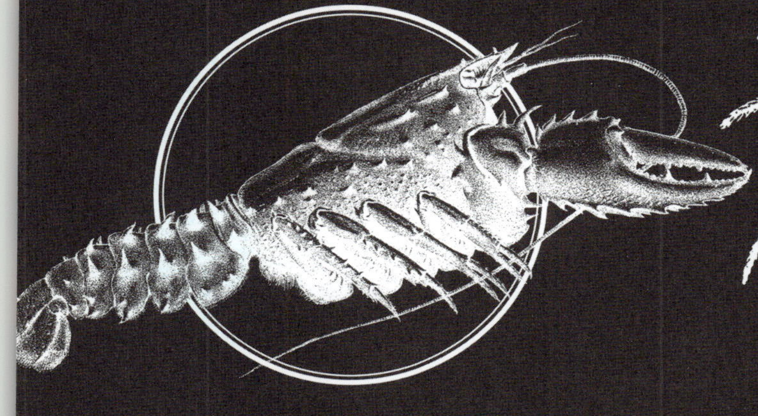

Murray crayfish This slow-growing Australian crayfish eventually reaches lengths of 9 inches after moulting several times.

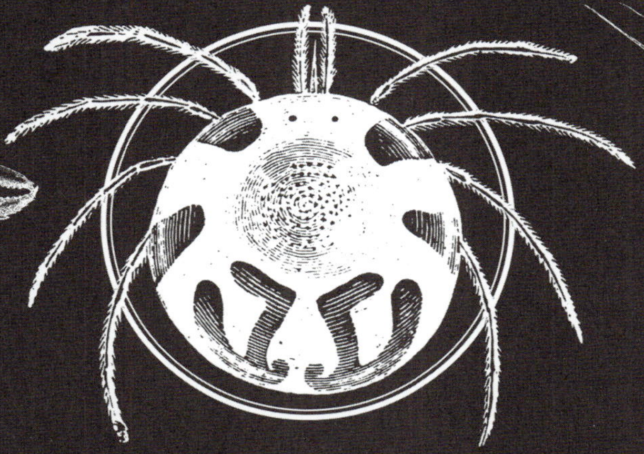

Water mite Adult water mites inject digestive juices into their prey with piercing mouthparts and then suck up the soupy insides.

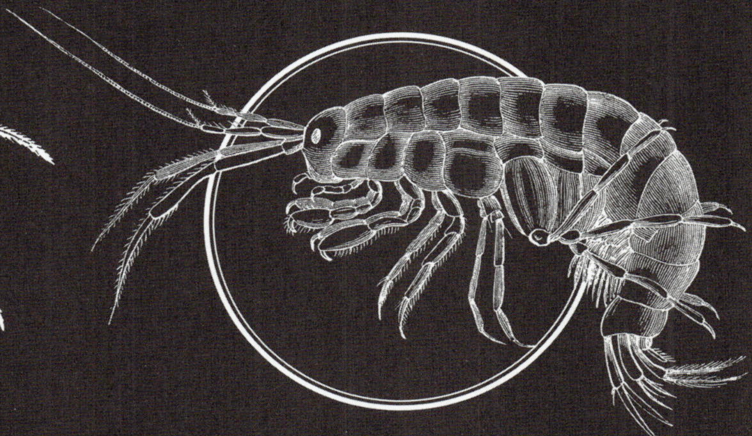

Freshwater shrimp Long antennae help this shrimp find decaying plant and animal material to eat. Gills on its legs take in oxygen from the water.

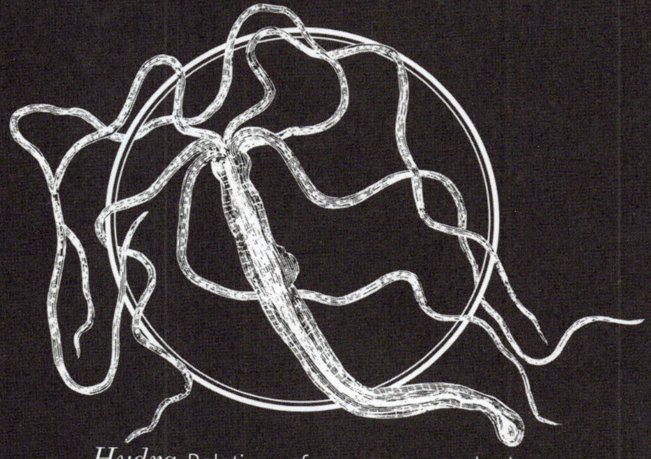

Hydra Relatives of sea anemones, hydra use stinging cells on their tentacles to catch small water animals. If threatened, they shrink into round blobs.

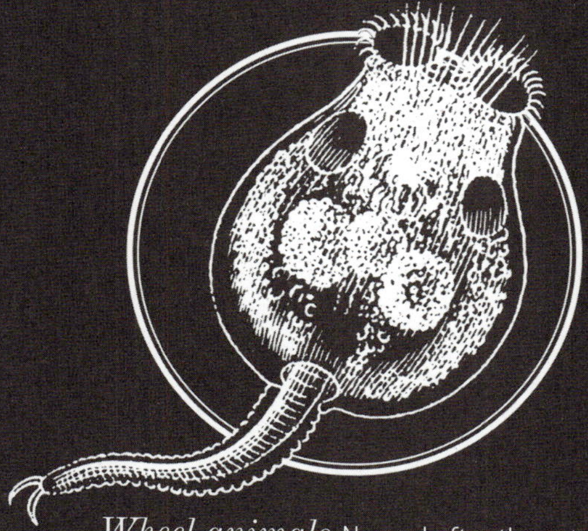

Wheel animals Named after the rotating "wheel" of tiny hair-like structures (cilia). These microscopic bugs use the "wheel" at their front end for moving and feeding.

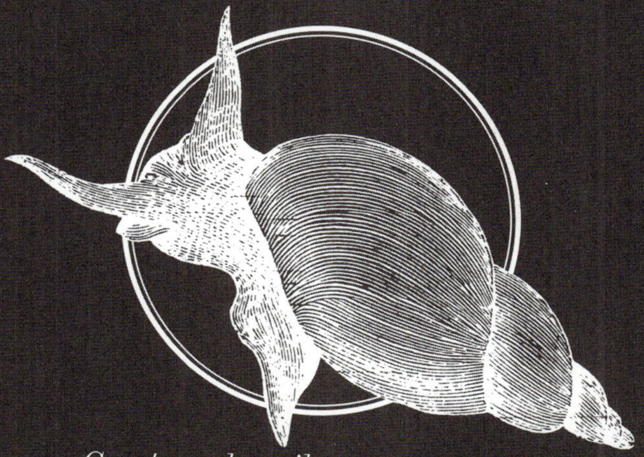

Great pond snail This snail swims to the surface to breathe air into its lungs and its large triangular tentacles help it to take in oxygen from the water.

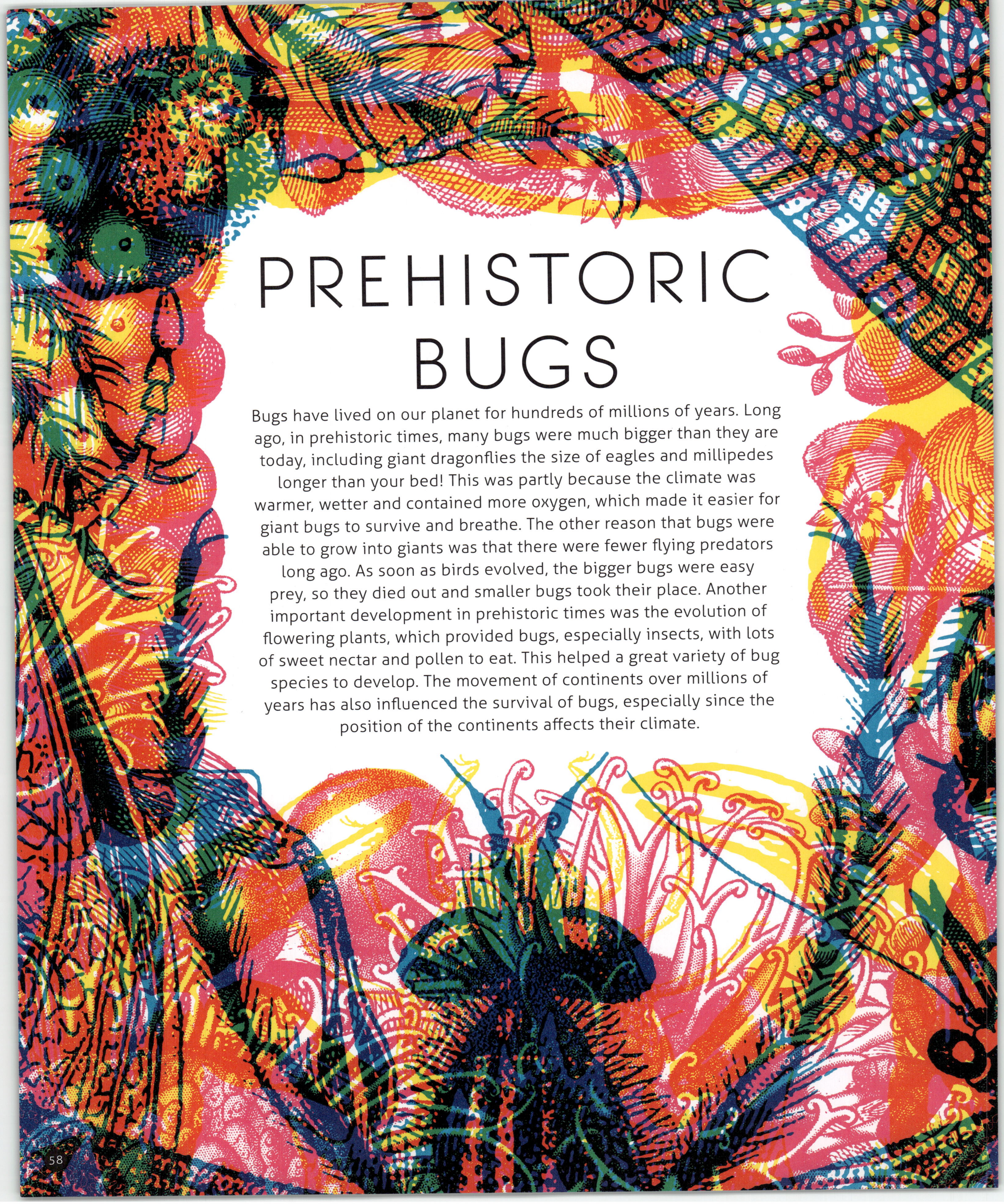

PREHISTORIC BUGS

Bugs have lived on our planet for hundreds of millions of years. Long ago, in prehistoric times, many bugs were much bigger than they are today, including giant dragonflies the size of eagles and millipedes longer than your bed! This was partly because the climate was warmer, wetter and contained more oxygen, which made it easier for giant bugs to survive and breathe. The other reason that bugs were able to grow into giants was that there were fewer flying predators long ago. As soon as birds evolved, the bigger bugs were easy prey, so they died out and smaller bugs took their place. Another important development in prehistoric times was the evolution of flowering plants, which provided bugs, especially insects, with lots of sweet nectar and pollen to eat. This helped a great variety of bug species to develop. The movement of continents over millions of years has also influenced the survival of bugs, especially since the position of the continents affects their climate.

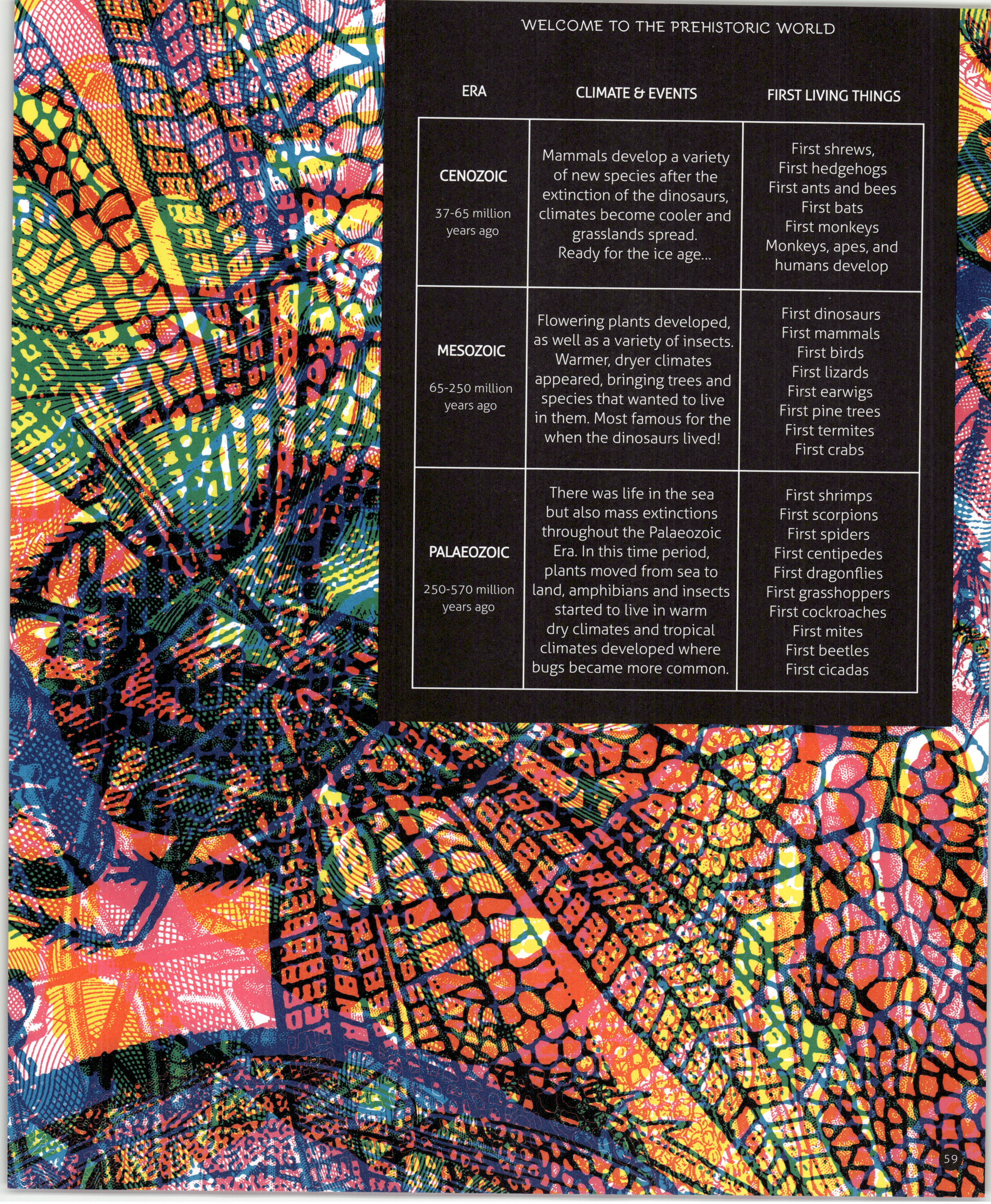

WELCOME TO THE PREHISTORIC WORLD

ERA	CLIMATE & EVENTS	FIRST LIVING THINGS
CENOZOIC 37-65 million years ago	Mammals develop a variety of new species after the extinction of the dinosaurs, climates become cooler and grasslands spread. Ready for the ice age...	First shrews, First hedgehogs First ants and bees First bats First monkeys Monkeys, apes, and humans develop
MESOZOIC 65-250 million years ago	Flowering plants developed, as well as a variety of insects. Warmer, dryer climates appeared, bringing trees and species that wanted to live in them. Most famous for the when the dinosaurs lived!	First dinosaurs First mammals First birds First lizards First earwigs First pine trees First termites First crabs
PALAEOZOIC 250-570 million years ago	There was life in the sea but also mass extinctions throughout the Palaeozoic Era. In this time period, plants moved from sea to land, amphibians and insects started to live in warm dry climates and tropical climates developed where bugs became more common.	First shrimps First scorpions First spiders First centipedes First dragonflies First grasshoppers First cockroaches First mites First beetles First cicadas

INSECTS

If you could travel back in time 100 million years, you would be able to watch a tiny, but deadly, cockroach as it stalked its prey right under the feet of the great dinosaurs. *Manipulator modificaputis* seized its prey in its long front legs, which were covered in strong spines, like a praying mantis. Its long neck allowed it to turn its head right round and it also had large eyes to spot predators. This was important because small dinosaurs no doubt enjoyed crunching up this mini-cockroach as a juicy night-time snack.

READ about the species below and then turn back to THE OBSERVATION DECK. Looking through the RED lens, what can you see?

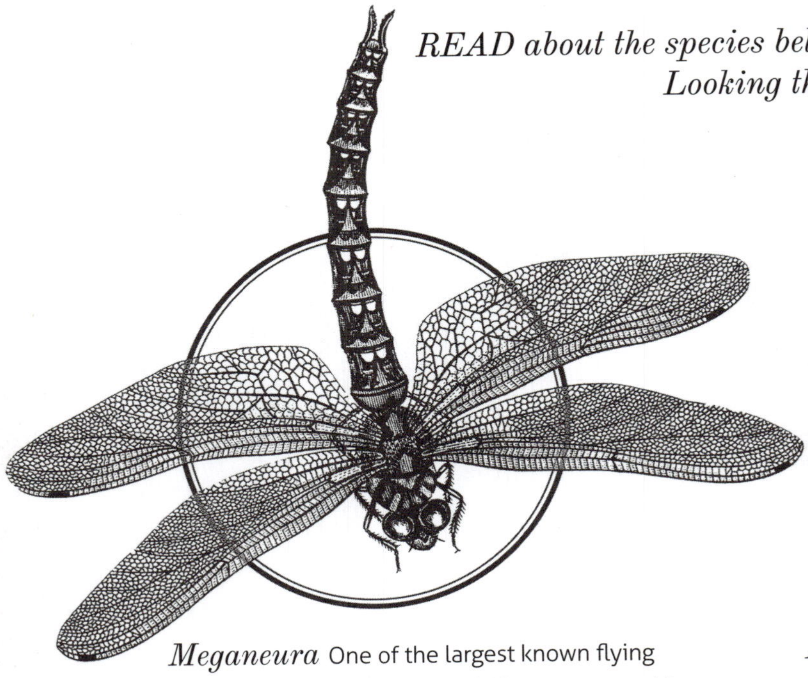

Meganeura One of the largest known flying insects of all time, eagle-sized *Meganeura* used its huge, strong wings and massive eyes to hunt for other insects and lizards.

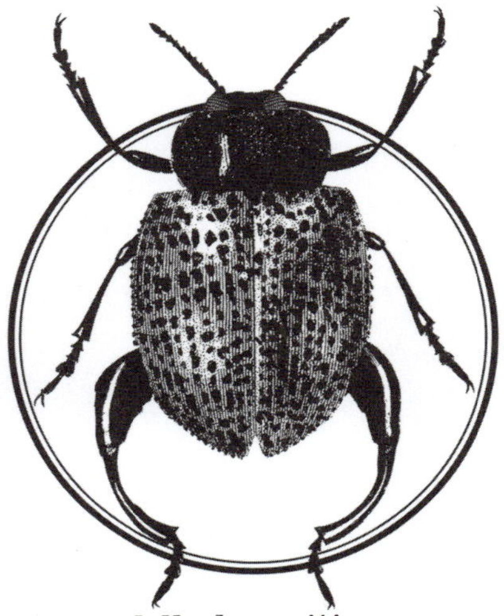

Angimordella burmitina This beetle, found preserved with pollen on its body and legs, may have been one of the first insects to carry pollen from one flower to another, nearly 100 million years ago.

Prodryas persephone The first fossil butterfly to be found in North America, *Prodryas* had short, brush-like front legs and is related to modern-day Admiral butterflies.

Raphidioptera Named after their long, snake-like "neck", snakeflies were much more varied and widespread in warmer dinosaur times but now live only in cooler places in the northern hemisphere.

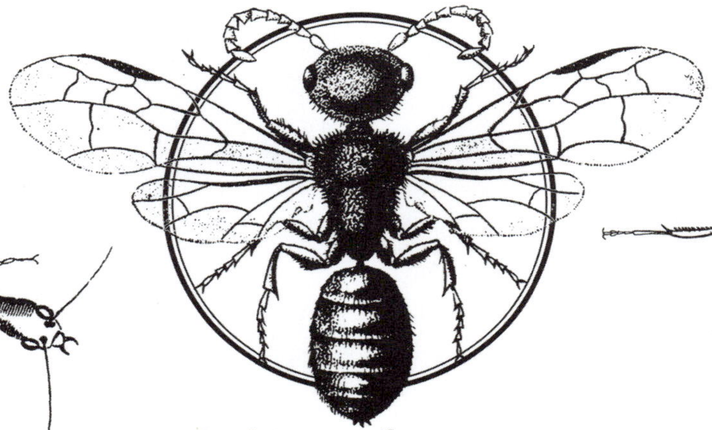

Brachyelatus marthae 40-million-year-old fossils of this tiny parasitic wasp were preserved in prehistoric amber, which is a sticky sap produced by conifer trees.

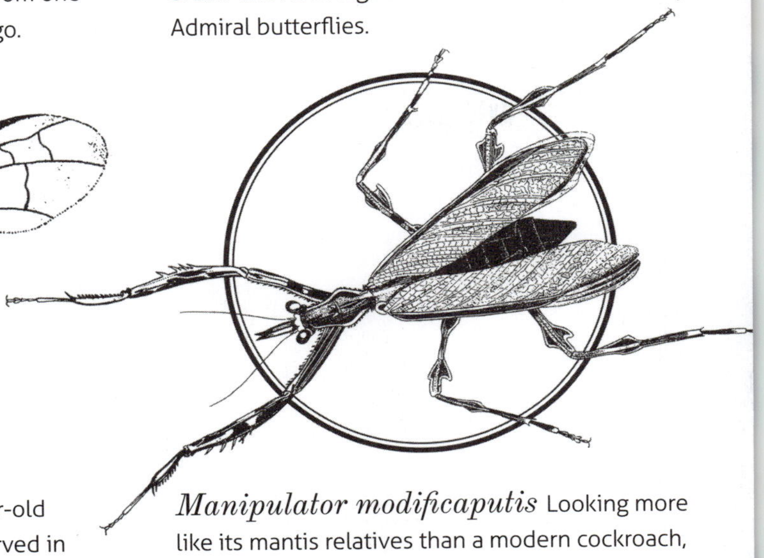

Manipulator modificaputis Looking more like its mantis relatives than a modern cockroach, this tiny bug probably hunted insect prey on the forest floor at night.

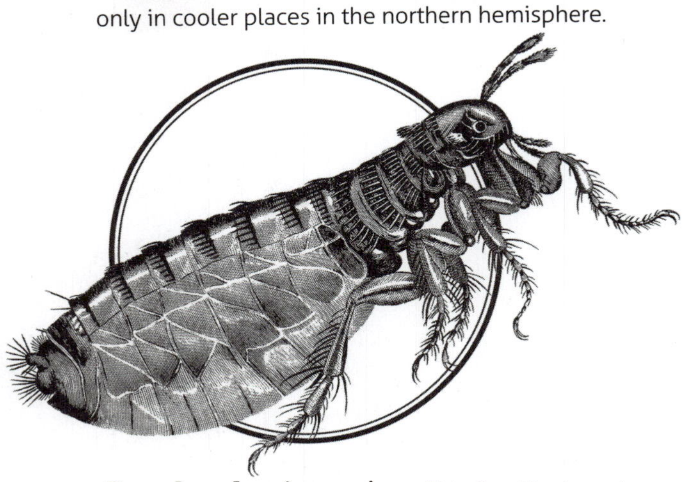

Pseudopulex jurassicus This flea-like insect used its jagged feeding tube to suck up the blood of dinosaurs, pterosaurs, and mammals. Long claws helped it to cling on to the animals while it was feeding.

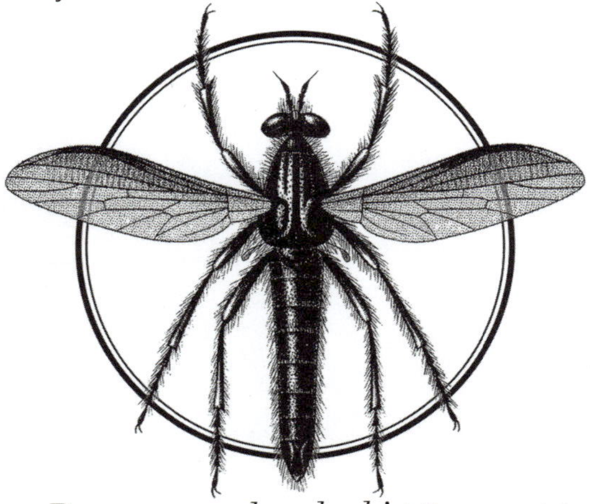

Burmapogon bruckschi A fierce predator, this assassin fly caught its prey in flight. It injected its prey with digestive juices, then sucked up their insides as a soupy meal.

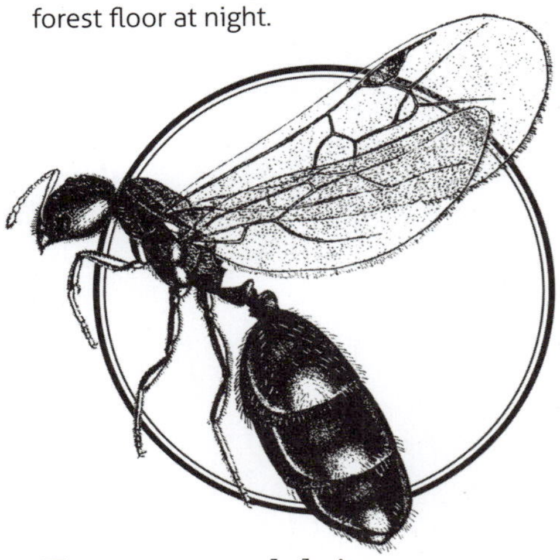

Titanomyrma lubei These giant ants probably lived in places with a tropical climate and had queen ants the size of hummingbirds or wrens.

OTHER CREEPY CRAWLIES

It is hard to believe that there were millipedes bigger than people scurrying through the swamp forests of North America some 300 million years ago. Yet truth is sometimes stranger than fiction! These giant creepy crawlies, called *Arthropleura*, were perhaps the largest land bugs of all time. They would have had few predators, so it is not surprising that their body armor was only a few millimeters thick. Arthropleura died out when the Earth's climate became drier and the lush forests where it lived were replaced by desert-like environments.

READ about the species below and then turn back to THE OBSERVATION DECK. Looking through the BLUE lens, what can you see?

Chimerachne yingi Like a spider, this bug had eight legs and could spin silk. But it also had a long, sensory tail, something that no living spider has.

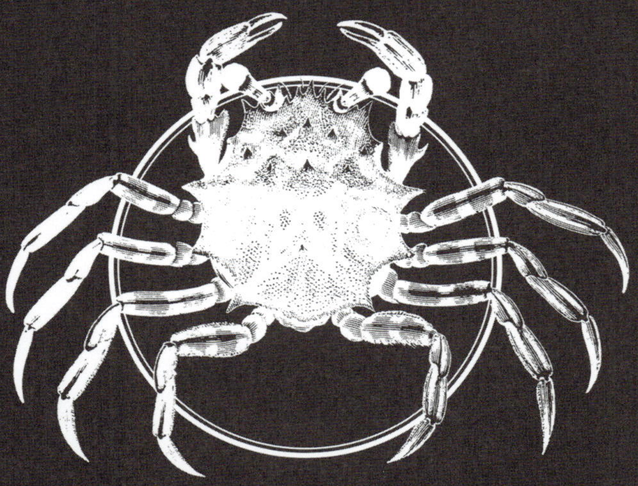

Cretapsara athanata This tiny crab had gills, not lungs, and may have been one of the first crabs to invade land and freshwater during dinosaur times.

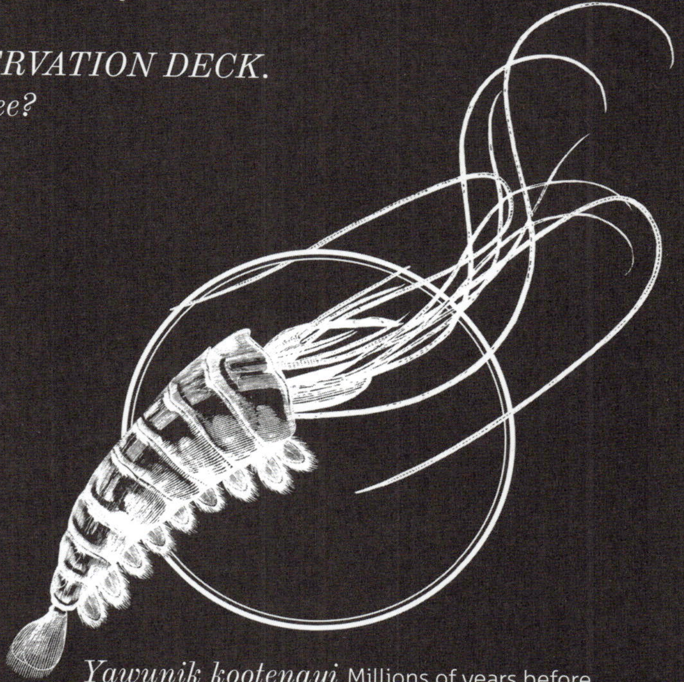

Yawunik kootenayi Millions of years before dinosaurs walked the Earth, this lobster-like creature lived in the oceans. It had three long claws and sensory whips on its head to catch prey.

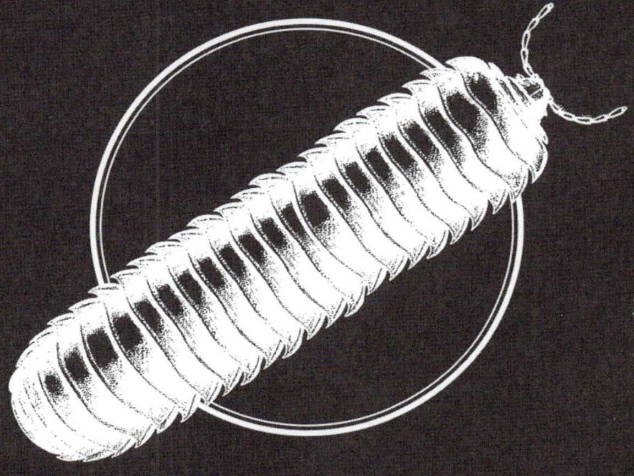

Arthropleura A distant relative of millipedes, Arthropleura used its strong jaws to chomp on swamp plants. The huge tracks left by its forty legs look like the tyre tracks from a vehicle.

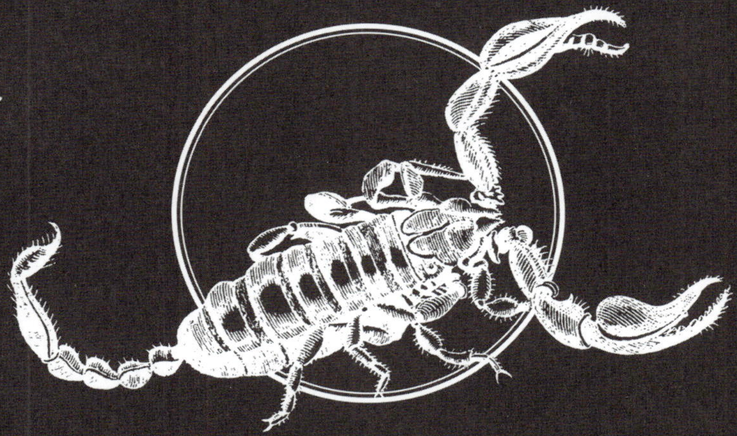

Pulmonoscorpius kirktonensis This giant scorpion measured 27 inches—twice the height of this book! It probably used the strong venom in its thick tail to overcome prey.

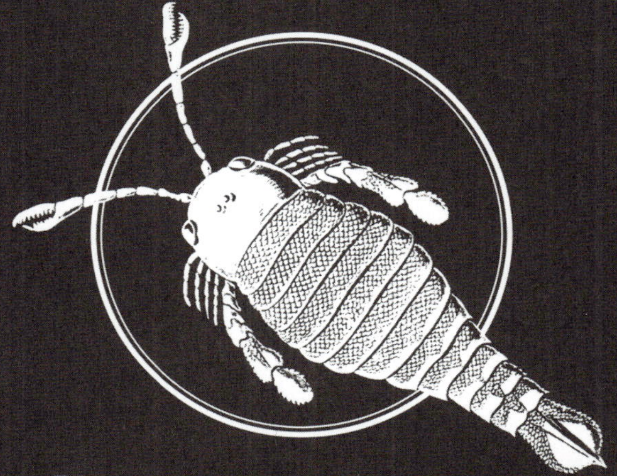

Pterygotus A human-sized "sea scorpion", Pterygotus was probably a night-time scavenger. It used its paddle-like legs for swimming and could flick its tail to provide extra speed.

Mongolarachne jurassica This large spider probably came out at night to catch prey in order to avoid daytime dinosaur hunters. It may have spun a woolly silk net to trap its meals.

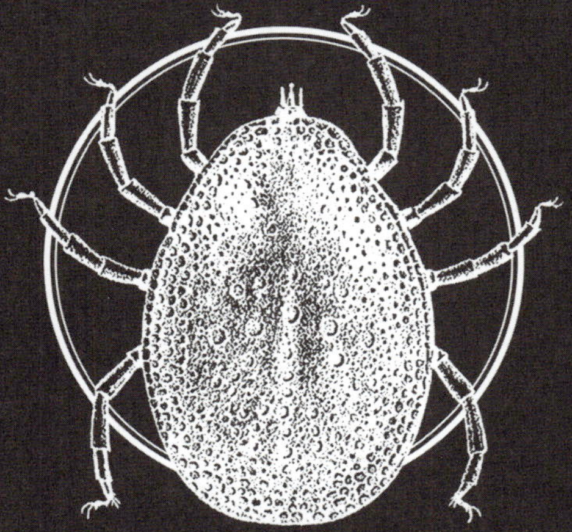

Deinocroton draculi An ancient tick that fed on the blood of feathered dinosaurs, *Deinocroton* was preserved among the remains of a 100 million-year-old dinosaur nest.

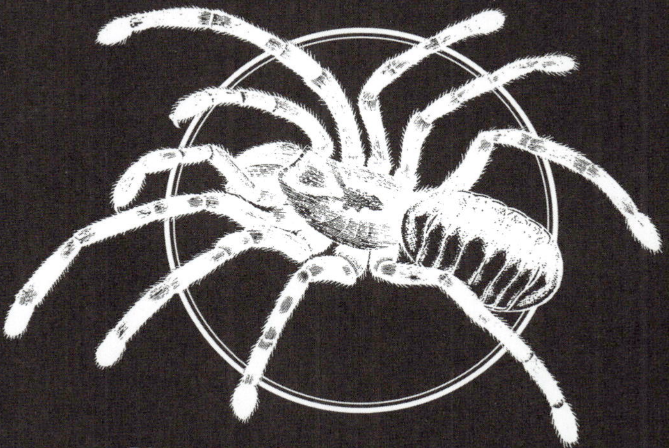

Idmonarachne brasieri Smaller than a postage stamp, this spider relative had eight legs and fangs but could not spin the silk it produced. It may have used the silk to line its burrows or wrap its eggs.

Scan the code to turn your device into a magic three color lens.

The Quarto Group
Inspiring | Educating | Creating | Entertaining

Brimming with creative inspiration, how-to projects, and useful information to enrich your everyday life, quarto.com is a favorite destination for those pursuing their interests and passions.

Author's note: The numbers of bug species quoted in this book are those available at the time this book was researched and written. These numbers increase every year as scientists discover and record new bug species all over the world.

First published in 2022 by Wide Eyed Editions, an imprint of The Quarto Group.
100 Cummings Center, Suite 265D, Beverly, MA 01915 USA.
T +1 978-282-9590 F +1 978-283-2742 www.Quarto.com

A catalogue record for this book is available from the British Library.

ISBN 978-0-7112-7512-6

The illustrations were created digitally
Set in Aller Light, Bellota and Old Standard

Published by Georgia Amson-Bradshaw
Designed by Lyli Feng
Commissioned by Lucy Brownridge
Project managed and edited by Poppy David
Production by Chris Tucker

Manufactured in ShaoGuan, China SL052022

9 8 7 6 5 4 3 2 1

FSC www.fsc.org MIX Paper | Supporting responsible forestry FSC® C122384